THE WAY OF A DISCIPLE

George Appleton has had a long, varied and adventurous ministry, beginning as a curate in Stepney in 1925, followed by nearly 20 years as a missionary in Burma, then as a parish priest in Harrow, after which he served for eight years as an ecumenical missionary secretary, gaining a knowledge of the worldwide Church and of other communities of faith. Five years as a City rector were followed by a short period as Archdeacon of London and Canon of St Paul's Cathedral. From that he was called to Western Australia to become Archbishop of Perth, and six years later pressed to become Anglican Archbishop in Jerusalem. Now in retirement he reflects on the discipleship which has been at the heart of this varied experience.

Bishop Appleton has been responsible for a number of books of prayers, many of them his own, and others which have stimulated and helped him to pray.

Books by the same author available in
Fount Paperbacks

JOURNEY FOR A SOUL

GEORGE APPLETON

The Way of a Disciple

With a Foreword by the
Archbishop of Canterbury

COLLINS
Fount Paperbacks
in association with
Faith Press

First published by Fount Paperbacks in association with
Faith Press in 1979

Made and printed in Great Britain by
William Collins Sons and Co. Ltd, Glasgow

Dedicated to

Bishop George West
Bishop of Rangoon, 1935–1954

in gratitude for fifty years of close friendship during which we talked many times
and exchanged many letters about the
meaning of discipleship

Contents

Foreword

Bishop George Appleton has been good to us. He has allowed us, as it were, to look over his shoulder and join with him as he has sat and meditated on the Scriptures. Better still, he has let us kneel with him and share his prayers as he turns his meditation God-wards.

Many will find this a lovely book and an immensely rewarding one. They will want to read it in a leisurely fashion – one section a day at the very most. To get the best from it, they will read it with their Bible open. As they do so, they will find their prayer-life enriched and deepened – the imagination will prove the road to the heart and the will.

George Appleton has had a long and fruitful ministry – and one of wide variety. He knows his East London, and his Far East. He has served in Australia and in Jerusalem. For more than half a century he has worked as priest and bishop, and all the time he has had his eyes up to God and his arms out to men. No wonder that his prayers have proved of help to many. This book, different in kind from his former ones but showing the same spiritual insight, will help many more. Thank you, dear Bishop.

DONALD CANTUAR:

Preface

The beginnings of this small book of devotions go back to my time in Western Australia, where I used to spend a quiet hour or so each day in the Chapel of Bishop's House. They were not first written down and then meditated upon, but came in the morning quiet and were written to preserve the memory and the inspiration.

When I was asked to write the Archbishop of Canterbury's Lenten Book for 1979, I remembered those meditations and was fortunate enough to find some of the notes, to which I have been able to add meditations throughout a year of preparation.

Those who have used the writings and prayers of others will recognize that there is not much of my own in this small book. They will recognize the debt I owe to the anonymous English writer of *The Cloud of Unknowing*, to Archbishop Temple, Archbishop Goodier, Father Teilhard de Chardin, and Dean Milner-White in particular, and also to a host of parish priests, writers, colleagues and friends, particularly Bishop George West, who have by their devotion and example taught me something of the meaning of discipleship.

There is much exercise of the mind in these devotional meditations. I hope there is also a suggestion of reflective, contemplative quiet, often in silence, when I waited, listened and received.

It will be recognized that a book of meditations is not designed to be read straight through, but taken one by one, and allowed to stimulate the contemplative faculty into quiet receptivity and interior communion.

I am grateful to Archbishop Donald for inviting me to write this small book. I cannot expect him, or any other user of it, to endorse every sentence, clause and word, though I hope that he will recognize a kindred devotion to the Lord of all disciples and a love of the Scriptures, both those which he studied so deeply and those which came from the experience of his earliest disciples.

John the Baptist's Day, 1978   G.A.

Biblical Quotations

In the quotations at the head of each chapter the various Bible translations or paraphrases used are indicated by initials, as follows:

A.V.   Authorized Version
J.B.   Jerusalem Bible
J.B.P. J. B. Phillips – New Testament in
        Modern English
L.B.   Living Bible
N.E.B. New English Bible
R.S.V. Revised Standard Version

PART I

The Master's Preparation

1. Answering a Call

Hebrews 10:7. *God, here I am! I am coming to obey your will.* (J.B.)

O Christ, my Lord, I thank you for confiding the experience of your baptism to your disciples. I can see the faith which led you to leave Nazareth, and its confirmation in the inner voice – 'Thou art my beloved Son', and the Father's happiness in your obedience. I can rejoice in your consciousness of the Spirit's power for the work ahead.

O God, grant that I too may obey your inner urgings, that I may weigh them and then in faith trust and obey them. Help me to feel that I too am a much-loved son and that your Spirit is available for all you want me to do. Grant me the confidence of knowing that you are pleased with my obedience, and help me to live as your son, sharing your nature and character, and doing your will, O Father of Jesus Christ and my Father.[1]

My dear Lord, the excited interest in John Baptist's fiery preaching must have reached Nazareth and been the signal to your waiting spirit. I can sense John's surprise when at the end of a long day's preaching, when the last conscience-aroused penitent had been washed in the water of Jordan, you came and stood before him. I can understand his reluctance to baptize you when in a flash of spiritual insight he recognized you as the Coming One about whom he had been preaching, the thong of whose sandals he said he was unworthy to stoop down and unloose.[2]

O Christ, my Lord, he recognized in you the one who could bring about an inner baptism of which his own bap-

1. Mark 1:9–11
2. Matthew 3:13–17

19

tizings were only a symbol and a hope, a baptism of forgiveness, spiritual rebirth and heavenly fire. Grant that all the baptizings of your Church may be of this nature, an inner effectiveness, whether immediate, gradual or long delayed in action.[3]

O Christ, my Lord, you stood in the water with the men of your time, identifying yourself with them in their sins, their penitence, their hopes. Help me to be fully human as you were, realizing my solidarity with them, not judging nor condemning, but seeking to understand, to pity and to help and even to excuse as you did when at the last you shared the fate of two poor criminals.

When I pray, O God, let heaven be open so that I may glimpse something of your glory and love, and feel that I belong to you. Let me feel the descent of the Spirit to strengthen me for all that you would have me be, and do, and hear. And help me follow where your well-beloved Son leads, keeping close to him. When I lag behind, let me see his footmarks and find him waiting for me around the next bend of faith, O loving Father of a well-beloved Son.

3. Luke 3:15–17; John 1:26–34

2. Seeking a Vocation

Mark 1:12. *The Spirit immediately drove him out into the wilderness.* (R.S.V.)

O Christ, my Lord, like Moses on Mount Sinai you spent forty days in the wilderness, thinking out in prayer and solitude how you should carry out the Father's will and how you should use the Spirit's power which you experienced welling up in you. Dear Lord, we talk of this time of retreat and preparation as the Temptation, as if the initiative was with the spirit of evil, whereas it was the Holy Spirit which so urgently moved you.[1]

I picture you, intent on the Father's will, when food and drink and human company were secondary to your desire to find out from the Father the way in which you should carry out the mission laid upon you. I see how certain suggestions came to your mind, which seemed initially good, with seeming support from Scripture, but which on closer examination proved to be subtle temptations to deviate from the Father's will and method.[2]

O Christ, my Lord, help me to bring everything to God. Save me from easy, superficial thinking, open my eyes to subtle temptations disguised as good. Let me not use what power I have for self-interest or to bribe people into the Kingdom; let me not seek wrong publicity or sensation or self-advertisement, nor to expect automatic, miraculous proof or intervention; let me not compromise with truth, integrity or love, but be whole-hearted in my commitment to you. Let me choose as you did, the way of love, service, sacrifice, knowing as you did that the Father will see us

1. Mark 1:12
2. Matthew 4:1–11; Luke 4:1–13

through difficulty, opposition, even death. And keep me conscious of the divine grace to support me when I choose your will.

Dear Lord, the forty days in the desert countryside were the first battle for the world's salvation, as critical as the last struggle in Gethsemane. Did you see at that earlier stage the shadow of the cross ahead, which became so clear and immediate in the garden of olives?

O Christ, all through your life you were tempted not only in the wilderness, with all the temptations common to human nature, so you know temptation's power. Grant me your insight to recognize temptation, and your grace to repel it. You shared our human nature, so you know the impulses, the strains, the desires and weaknesses. You resisted temptation to the full, so you know its power better than we do who succumb before its most critical moment. You are able to rescue, encourage and strengthen us. We come in hopeful and grateful confidence to you, to find grace to help in time of need, and divine light to guide us to recognize the Father's purpose for the life of each, and the advancement of his Kingdom.[3]

3. Hebrews 4:15

3. Finding a Gospel

Luke 4:18. *The Spirit of the Lord is upon me, because he has anointed me to preach good news to the poor.* (R.S.V.)

O Christ, my Lord, it was on your first visit to Nazareth after your experience down by the Jordan, that you explained the heart of the Gospel that you felt commissioned to preach. Not a message of stern condemnation like many of the prophets, or like John Baptist's warning of fiery judgement to which you had listened. Doubtless news of the happenings at the Jordan had reached your home, and the villagers would want to hear about them from your own lips. Also on the way back you had preached in the synagogues of Galilee, so it was natural that you should be invited to preach in the synagogue where you had so often worshipped and where the call from the Father had stirred within your spirit.[1]

O Christ, my Lord, I marvel at your knowledge of your Bible which enabled you to pick out your text from Isaiah 61. I marvel still more at the application of these words to your own ministry, gracious words, as the hearers remarked. The anointing of the Spirit so recently, was so that you could take good news to the poor, the poor in worldly wealth and the humble of spirit: good news that God loves, God cares, God forgives, God comes. Good news too that all in the Kingdom will want to create conditions where all shall care for each and each for all.

There is to be release to the prisoners of sin, fear and despair, relief to the heavy-burdened and oppressed, for you will be their yoke-fellow for every burden. You will

1. Luke 4:16–21; Isaiah 61:1–2

23

bring sight to the inly blind, and help the physically blind to overcome their handicap, with the fellowship of your Church to care for them. Your coming is truly a year of jubilee when all pledges must be given back, all debts cancelled, all slaves freed, according to the Law of the Lord.

O Christ, my Lord, shall men's hearts be so changed by your coming into our life and into our world that these things shall happen? It is already being fulfilled in some measure.

I marvel again, my Lord, that you left out part of the Scripture you chose: you omitted the words 'and the day of vengeance of our God', for your message was a Gospel of love and forgiveness. You had the deep conviction that the Father had sent you not to condemn the world, but that the world through you might be saved. O gracious God-spelling Lord![2]

O Christ, my Lord, I pray that the Church may take these words to itself and be your collective Gospel, carrying on the ministry worded for you by that prophet in ruined Jerusalem 600 years earlier.

2. Isaiah 61:2; John 3:16–17

4. Opening Message

Mark 1:15. The time has come at last – the Kingdom of God has arrived. You must change your hearts and minds and believe the good news. (J.B.P.)

O Christ, my Lord, the earliest memories of you tell us that your first preaching was centred on the Kingdom of God. A new era had dawned in which the hopes of the past would be fulfilled. In one sense it was like the return of your people from exile, with the way being made straight, level and smooth. In another sense it was like the coming of a divine messenger who would cleanse both the ministers and the worship of the Temple.[1]

In still another sense, dear Lord, your teaching about the Kingdom was a continuation of the divine Law given originally on Sinai, and expanded and dispersed in succeeding generations. The Law of the Lord and the Rule of the Kingdom must have been very close in your thinking; I pray that Jews and Christians may study their connection.

O Christ, my Lord, you insisted that the good news that the Kingdom of God was at hand demanded a double response from your hearers – a change of heart, a new outlook, new thinking, new attitudes, and a clear, simple, joyful acceptance of the good news. I accept, dear Lord, that the Kingdom is the sovereignty of God in the hearts and the affairs of people, both individual and corporate. I see that I must put my life under the rule of God, obey the first and greatest of all the commandments of the Torah, the divine Law, which is the treasure of your first people, Israel, to love God with all my being, putting him first in my life. Then I realize that I shall be free from all lesser loyalties, I

1. Mark 1:14–15; Luke 3:4–6; Malachi 3:1–3

shall be whole.[2]

You tell me that the Kingdom is like a seed, with germinating power, with growth as great as any seed in nature – thirty-, sixty-, a hundred-fold. All you ask from me is an honest and good heart into which you can drop your seed. You tell me that the seed must be buried in the soil of the heart, nourished by faith and love, until the day it bursts through the surface and grows into a root of corn for nourishment or a tree for shelter.[3]

You add, dear Lord, that the Kingdom is like a treasure, which some stumble on by accident and others find after a long search. Then gently and lovingly you insist that I must give everything I have to secure it.[4]

O Christ, my Lord, 'Thy Kingdom Come!' – in my heart, in the world in which I live, so that all may enjoy its creativity and blessedness.

2. John 3:5–6
3. Mark 4:1–8, 26–30
4. Matthew 13: 44–6

5. Always a Jew

Matthew 5:17. *Do not suppose that I have come to abolish the Law and the prophets; I did not come to abolish, but to complete.* (N.E.B.)

O Christ, my Lord, you were born a Jew, you lived as a Jew, you died as a Jew. Your parents observed the usual customs of birth and infancy; you participated in the Passover, attended the great festivals, joined in the worship of the synagogue, taught in both the synagogue and the Temple. You said that you had come to fulfil the Law, not to abolish it, you believed that your people had a special part in God's saving purpose.[1]

You hold the whole human race in your heart, as Abraham did. You chose twelve apostles to parallel the twelve tribes and you sent them out to the world. You fed the people in the wilderness as Moses did. Like Isaiah you wanted the Temple to be a place of prayer for all nations. It looks, dear Lord, as if your ancient people and your new people were meant to work together. Your servant Paul was equally convinced of his Jewishness, and tried to keep Jewish and Gentile disciples together.[2]

All your teaching, dear Master, was given in a Jewish setting which we need to understand if we want to see your relevance and significance. We often speak of getting back to you as a historical figure, but many of us find this difficult. Perhaps we need to study afresh your Jewishness. We know how you studied and loved your Hebrew Scriptures and believed that you had come to fulfil them, not to do away

1. Luke 2:21, 27, 42; Mark 14:12–17; Matthew 5:17; John 4:22
2. Genesis 12:2; Isaiah 56:7; Mark 11:17

with them. Without them we cannot understand either you or the Father. Yet we also know, dear Jewish Jesus, how you loved both the Law and the Prophets, and how you gave them wider, deeper, truer meaning.

You loved the earthly Jerusalem, dear Lord, and we can never forget the analogy of your love as a hen sheltering her chicks under her wings. You wept over its failure to be the City of God and the centre of peace. You felt that your death would have its greatest effect if it took place in Jerusalem.[3]

A Jewish disciple saw the earthly Jerusalem as meant to represent the heavenly Jerusalem, 'the mother of us all', the eternal home of the human spirit. Yet you so clearly saw its need of reform, and you pictured true worship as marked by spirit and truth.

You had your Jewish friends, even in these last days of human tragedy – the eleven confused but faithful disciples, the even more faithful women, the man whose donkey you borrowed, the man who guided you to the Upper Room, the women of Jerusalem who wept as you were led to execution, Joseph of Arimathaea and Nicodemus, member of the Sanhedrin, who gave your body honourable burial. O dear Lord, it was only a powerful minority that plotted and shouted for your death. And the first three thousand members of your Church were all your own people.[4]

O Christ, my Lord, forgive us Gentile Christians that we have treated your people so cruelly, holding your death unforgivably against them, in spite of your first prayer from the cross. Forgive us for assuming that since the separation between us, we have claimed their place entirely, and regarded them as spiritually dead and ineffective.

O dear Christ, I thank you that your original people and we your later followers are again beginning to talk together about you. Lead us into truth, help us both to see the Father's will for our relationship today, so that we can

3. Luke 13:34
4. Mark 11:3, 14:13–18; Luke 23:27; John 19:38–47

work together for the world's salvation, for which you lived and died and rose indestructible. O Christ, my Lord, I see you in both the Jewish Jesus and the Christ of Christian faith. Let me be disciple to both.

PART II
Calling Disciples

6. Two Pairs of Brothers

Revelation 2:17. *I will give him also a white stone,
and on the stone will be written a new name,
known to none but him that receives it.* (N.E.B.)

O Christ, my Lord, the men you first called were fishermen,
and you told them that in future they were to catch men. You
took over at least two from John the Baptist, directed to you
by him. What did you say to them in those first hours
together that so convinced them? Speak to me, O Lord,
that I may make my commitment and speak of you to
others with quiet, natural confidence, not in a professional
way but as introducing a new friend to old friends.

O Christ, you seemed to look right into Peter and see his
lovableness and instability, the sand of his character needing
to be fused into sandstone. Do you look at me and see
what I am, and what under you I might become? Do you
give me a new name?[1]

Do you look at each man's work and see how it can be
used for the Kingdom? – a teacher to teach truth with
patience, and develop character in his pupils; an accountant
to stand for honest and wise use of money; a shop assistant
to serve people courteously and resourcefully; a dressmaker
to make things for customers to suit their shape and
character; a priest to stand before God for people, and
before people for God?[2]

O Christ, I am not much good in catching men, either by
net or by hook and line. Give me patience and skill, let me
study each one so that I may begin where he is. Let me

1. John 1:35–42; Mark 1:16–20; Luke 5:1–11; Revelation
2:17
2. 1 Corinthians 12:4–11

catch him for you and for his own great benefit, and not for my satisfaction or professional efficiency.

Teach me, Lord. Be with me wherever I go, and show me the meaning of things, the real needs of people and the way to serve them.

Lord, let me be a learner in your school, accept your values, watch you at work, learn your ways and share your love. O Christ, my Lord, you tell me that all I have to do is to follow you. Sometimes you are near and present, and to follow is easy. Sometimes you are ahead, and I am timid and unwilling. Sometimes you are even out of sight. At such times, Lord, let me be confident that all I have to do is to follow in faith, knowing that you will come back to find me, so that we can travel along together again.

7. Two Friends

Matthew 18:3. *Unless you change your whole outlook and become like little children you will never
enter the Kingdom of Heaven.*   (J.B.P.)

O Christ, my Lord, the evangelists tell us so little of your
life among men, so few details of each incident. I want to
know what passed between you and Philip when you first
met, and all that I am told is that ultimately you called him
to follow you. Perhaps that is all I need to know, all that I
need to do.

Was Philip a man of few words, not clever and per-
suasive in argument, whose only thought was to get
people to you so that they could judge for themselves? Was
he so slow in perception that he needed everything spelled
out for him, as you seem to suggest in your gentle reproof
that it was taking a long time for him to perceive that you
show us God? I thank you, O Lord, for your patience with
him, which gives me hope that you are patient with me
also.

He brought Nathaniel to you, quickly after his own first
attraction to you. Lord, you saw deep into Nathaniel, as
you saw into Peter a few days earlier. You saw a man of
childlike spirit, without any guile, a Jacob without Jacob's
twist which took so long to straighten out.

O Lord, the angels could come down upon the spirit of
sleeping Jacob, the mother-spoilt son, the deceiver of his
brother, yet with spiritual potential and hope. The traffic
between the spiritual sphere and the human sphere can be
so much more easy, immediate, effective, in a man like
Nathaniel Bartholomew. Christ my Lord, give me the
childlike spirit that I may see the Kingdom and enter it, and
find in it the priceless treasure that never loses its value.

Calling Disciples

Let me follow with Philip and his friend, to be trained in your school, and become, in time, a member of your staff, O Christ, my Lord and Master.

John 1:43–51, 6:5–7, 12:20–22, 14:8–11; Genesis 28:10–17; Matthew 18:1–4; Luke 10:21

8. Unexpected Choice

1 Corinthians 1:28. *Those whom the world thinks common and contemptible are the ones that God has chosen – those who are nothing at all.* (J.B.)

O Christ, my Lord, here again I would like to know more of your earliest contacts with Matthew. Did he stroll down to the lakeside in quiet times at his taxpost and listen to your teaching, your parables about the Kingdom, so many of which are collected in his gospel? Did you talk with him at his post? Whatever the first contacts, you saw in him a potential follower, a man of promise. His indirect work for the Romans, his low place in social circles, were no obstacle to you. Perhaps he voiced his need for spiritual help and cure. Lord, you said you could do much for people who know they are in need, who realize the need of cure and change within their own souls. Prescribe for me, for I want to be whole and holy and loving.

Don't let me be ashamed to speak of you to my friends, those in my own sphere, or to speak simply and naturally about you. Let me so value what you do for me, that I may want others to meet you as I would want to introduce a newly-found friend to old friends.

Dear Lord, let me be as interested in your teaching as Matthew was. Let me study and implement your sermon on the hillside, when you laid down the principles of the Kingdom, and the character you wanted in your followers, your aim that we should move towards the perfection of God, your Father and ours. Help me to know the things that bring inner blessing; help me to see that motive and desire must be Christified, so that character and behaviour may be sanctified. Give me your mind, O Christ my Lord, so that I never despise anyone, but look through your eyes and see their potentiality for disciplehood and their value in working for the Kingdom.

Mark 2:13–17; Matthew 9:9–13; Luke 15:1–7

9. A Tragic Mistake?

Luke 23:34. *Father, forgive them; they do not know
what they are doing.*   (N.E.B. and J.B.)

O Christ, my Lord, you prayed all night before you chose
your twelve disciples, and then you chose Judas to be one of
them. You must have seen great possibilities in him. Even
when you knew he was not heart-whole in his loyalties you
still hoped, and at the Supper gave him the sop. You
washed his feet, a gesture of friendship and honour. You did
not denounce him before the others. You believed that what
he was doing would be taken up into the purpose of the
Father.

O Christ, what made him betray you? Did he want to
force your hand, make you declare yourself as Messiah, use
your power as you were tempted to do in the wilderness
retreat? O Lord, I know he was a free agent, that he was not
predestined to betray you, any more than I am. O Lord,
need he have taken the thirty pieces of silver? Could it have
been part of his technique to make you act with power, to
ensure that the rulers would act? Even if he did have this
plan in mind, it was a self-willed act, a tragic misunderstanding of you and your will. But was the kiss of betrayal
necessary? Was his greeting 'Hail, Master', the base
treachery that it has always seemed?

Whatever his motive, mistaken, deluded or treacherous,
you took it up into your purpose, accepted it. Yet your reply
to it suggests that it was real betrayal.

O Christ, could there have been any greater punishment
than to realize his complete mistake, his tragic self-will? Was
there any element of expiation in his suicide? Or was it just
despair, remorse, a shame which could not weep and ask
for forgiveness as Peter did? Dear Lord, you alone know.

When you hung upon the cross you must have thought of poor Judas. Did you have him in mind also when you promised the thief that you would be with him in Paradise? Did you seek out Judas as you both joined the ranks of the dead? O Lord, I pray that you did and that he was humble enough to accept your forgiveness.

O Christ, I ask with the other eleven, 'Is it I?' for I do not want to betray you knowingly and wilfully. Grant that I may be heart-whole in my loyalty, even though, like the others, I am weak, cowardly and confused. Let me humbly and lovingly accept your forgiveness, and with your love and help be a heart-whole follower, so that I can in some degree fulfil the hope you had when you called me.

Luke 6:12–16; Mark 14:17–21; John 13:21–30; Luke 22:47–48; Matthew 27:1–5

10. The Twelve

1 Corinthians 1:26. *Notice among yourselves, dear brothers, that few of you who follow Christ have big names or power or wealth.* (L.B.)

O Christ, my Lord, did you choose the twelve to extend the people of God to the whole world, to fulfil the divine promise to Abraham so that all nations should be blessed through him, to renew the covenant of Sinai that Israel should be a nation of priests to the world? They were to be with you, to be taught and trained, to watch you at work, to share your mind and outlook. At first you sent them out to Israel only, to pass on your Gospel that the Kingdom of God had come. You authorized them to heal the sick in body and mind. You told them that they were to trust in God alone and that they were to seek out the lost sheep. You warned them that there would be opposition, but that they would be given the right word in each situation. They were very ordinary people, none of them wealthy or from leading families, or rabbinically trained. Their faith in you was to be their most important qualification. You were clearly pleased, dear Lord, when Peter, speaking for them all, confessed you as Messiah.[1]

They were often slow of heart to learn the lessons you taught, they quarrelled over who should be the greatest. Yet all, save one, were deeply troubled when you disclosed that you knew that one of them would betray you. You were grateful to them for continuing with you through your difficulties and trials, though at the critical moment in Gethsemane even the intimate three failed to give you the

1. Matthew 10:1–8, 19–20; Mark 8:27–31

support you so deeply hoped for.[2]

In the Upper Room you called them friends, having shared with them the Father's mind and purpose, and in your great prayer you implicitly thanked God that they had received the word you spoke to them from him.[3]

Only one stood at the foot of your cross, but two days later they were still together, though in fear lest they should meet a similar fate to yours. With the cross of love behind you they received the command to world mission when in Easter joy and confidence they heard you say, 'As the Father sent me, so I send you,' and when you breathed into them the love and power of the Spirit, in which they were to move out into the world with a Gospel of love and forgiveness.[4]

Because of their obedience I am your disciple today, dear Master and Lord. Keep me humble, loving and faithful. Let me be often in your company, learning your mind, seeking your guidance, accepting your encouragement, patient under your reproof, eager for your will. You have shown me the Father, dear Lord, in terms of a human life, and through you I have access to him.

Lord, there will be times when my faith is low and my love lukewarm, when the scepticism of men shakes me. At such times, dear Master, I will say with those first disciples, 'Lord, to whom else shall we go?' You have the secret of eternal life, and I believe that you are the Holy One of God.[5]

2. Luke 22:24–30
3. John 15:15, 17:6–8
4. John 19:26, 20:19–23
5. John 6:66–69

PART III

Training Disciples

11. The Values of the Kingdom

Matthew 5:3–10. *Happy are those who know their need . . . who know what sorrow means . . . who claim nothing . . . who are hungry and thirsty for true goodness . . . the merciful . . . the utterly sincere . . . those who make peace . . . who have suffered persecution for the cause of goodness.*
(J.B.P.)

O Christ, my Lord, I see the character that you want in your followers, the character which alone can bring your blessedness.

Grant that I may be poor in spirit, detached from worldly possessions, conscious of my need, humble in gratitude for your gifts. Grant that I may mourn over the sorrows and sins of others, so that I may realize the strength of your comfort and the joy of your forgiveness.

Help me to be meek, to be free from all pride, self-assertion, all desire for recognition and praise. Let me never put myself forward. Let me gladly take the lowest place and not expect to be invited to go higher. Let me be humble, sensitive, free from any self-seeking, grateful to be included among your followers.

Grant that I may have a passionate desire for righteousness – for truth in mind and honesty in action, working always for your will. Make this desire for your Kingdom as strong as a hungry man's desire for food or a thirsty man's longing for water.

Lord, make me merciful towards others, never judging or condemning their sins, but sorrowing for them. Let me be compassionate when people are in trouble, quick to help. Yet let me not lose the passion for righteousness, nor the resistance of love to all that falls below the standards of your Kingdom.

Make me single-hearted, whole-hearted in my devotion to you, making you the great reality of my life, my chief good, with no compromise or subtle self-seeking, so that I may see you in the glory and love of the Father.

O Christ, give me peace of heart in the assurance of your love, forgiveness and grace, make me peaceable in all my relationships. Help me to bring peace to all I meet, and to strive lovingly for peace among men. Help me to see the things that make for peace and those that make for division and war. Remove from my heart all aggressive motives, and help me to strive for peace in my own nation and in its attitudes to other nations.

Let me not be surprised or hurt if my loyalty to you arouses resentment in the minds and actions of others who do not yet have that loyalty. Let me see that evil will always resent goodness and that therefore I cannot expect the approval of everyone. Let me not expect any other treatment than that which people gave to you.

O Christ, my Lord, help me to gain this character, to have your mind, and so receive the blessedness which you promise to all whose aim it is to follow you.

Matthew 5:1–11; Luke 6:20–23; Galatians 5:22–23; James 3:17–18

12. Hidden Effectiveness

Matthew 5:13. *You are the world's seasoning, to make it tolerable. If you lose your flavour, what will happen to the world?* (L.B.)

O Christ, my Lord, you tell me that I am to work in hidden ways like salt, giving tone and flavour to the environment in which I am placed, keeping things from going rotten, and losing myself in doing so. Let me not be insipid and colourless, let me have the salty tang of your Kingdom. Renew my saltiness when it loses its power. Let my words have the touch of truth, the tang of challenge about them.

You tell me also that I am to be like yeast, fermenting the little circle in which I live and work. Let each community of your followers have this leavening influence, in the attitudes, the thinking, the creativity of their local society.

Yet in another way, you tell me that we must be noticeable like light, making things clear, as obvious as a light in a dark place or a city on a hill visible from a distance. The character of our lives, the imaginative quality of our actions, must stand out. Our light comes from you. We are only the lamp. Shine through us, O Lord, that men may recognize the source of our light and want it for themselves.

Let the Church be the light of the world, helping men to see the perils, the tragedies, the problems, the opportunities, and then to shed your light upon them so that they may know what needs to be done.

Help us to recognize and welcome light wherever it shines, knowing that your operation is not our monopoly. Gather up all glimmers of light, all broken lights, into your

47

central glow, so that the Church may be like you, the light
of the world.

Matthew 5:13–16, 13:33; Luke 14:34; Colossians 4:6

13. Deep in the Heart

Proverbs 23:26. *My son, give me your heart, and let your eyes observe my ways.* (R.S.V.)

O Christ, my Lord, when you gathered your first followers you told them that in your coming the Kingdom of God had drawn near, so good and creative that it demanded a change of heart, a new outlook, a personal revolution. When you talked of the Kingdom was it another way of speaking of the Law of the Lord so dear to your own people?

You came not to abolish or destroy but to perfect and fulfil. You took the old commands down into the depths of thought and motive. It is not enough not to kill, we must get rid of the motives, feelings, attitudes, which lead to murder – anger, contempt of others, thinking of them as useless and without value, so easily expendable.

Your followers must not be content with avoiding gross sexual sin, they must deal with lust in the imagination, they must discipline the eyes. We must not be content with telling the truth on oath, we must always speak the truth, so that an oath is never needed. Our answers must be a plain 'yes' or 'no', without compromise or evasion.

O Lord, you do indeed fulfil the old Law, you bring out its full meaning in thought, motive and attitude. You make it much more demanding and challenging. You will not accept lip-service, literal observance, compromise. You demand that we shall be perfect, as God is.

O Christ, our Lord, how can we ever attain to such a standard? We must always fall short of your will and your glories, we are always unprofitable servants.

Yet you say the Kingdom of God is here, that it is possible for God to rule our minds and hearts and wills. You show us this in your own person, and you promise that the pupil shall become as his teacher.

O Christ, my Lord, you are present with everyone, an omnipresence of which your local presence two thousand years ago was the prototype. You are incarnate in each faithful follower, the companion, guide, encourager of my spirit. I want your outlook, your character, your mind, your way of life. Teach me, show me, help me.

Matthew 5:17–37; Luke 6:40; Matthew 10:24–25; James 5:12; Proverbs 23:26

14. Motives for Piety

Matthew 6:6. *When you pray, go into a room by yourself, shut the door, and pray to your Father who is there in the secret place.* (N.E.B.)

O Christ, my Lord, you teach your followers how to pray and you are insistent that we should have the right motives in prayer. I see that if I pray ostentatiously with the hope of getting a reputation for piety, I shall in all probability get that reputation. But that will be all the value of my prayer. It will not be acceptable to you nor will it have the real effect. My prayer must be humble, a secret between you and me, with the aim of the Father's glory and the doing of his will.

Let my prayer be simple and direct, without too much speaking. I do not need to tell you all the facts or diagnose each person's need or advise you what to do. You know everyone's needs, you understand every situation. I express my concern and ask that your wisdom and love may act. You love every soul, more even than I love my loved ones. Your will for them is better than I can imagine, describe or ask. Let me bring people to you in prayer, simply and lovingly invoking your grace for them.

You tell me that my giving must be secret, without any ulterior motive of appearing generous or seeking praise. I remember another word of yours which tells me that right giving brings an interior blessedness, giving more happiness than receiving. O Lord, I like receiving thoughtful, loving gifts, they warm the heart. Can it really be that giving produces even deeper happiness?

You tell me that discipline and austerity must be practised but again you warn me not to exercise them to attract the praise of others. It is safer, you say, to appear to be keeping festival, so that unhindered by my wrong motives, you can work within me, sanctifying, amorizing, toughening.

O Christ, my Lord, cleanse me in the secret hidden depths of my being, so that I may pray rightly, give unselfconsciously and discipline all my motives and desires which you alone know. Then Lord, keep at work within me, so that I may be a faithful student of your ways, under training to carry out your will.

Matthew 6:1–16; Psalm 51:6–12; Acts 20:35

15. The True Treasure

Matthew 6:21. *For where your treasure is, there will your heart be also.* (A.V.)

O Christ, my Lord, you tell me to consult my heart to discover what my most valued treasure is. To what person or object do my thoughts most frequently fly? You warn me that worldly treasures are subject to theft or natural deterioration. The things I value most must be those of the spirit.

You tell me that the values of the spirit are worth giving everything to get, that they alone bring lasting satisfaction. O Christ, let me seek the pearls of divine wisdom, until at length I discover the pearl of great price and give all that I have to possess it. Let me be on the look-out for spiritual treasure. Let me be grateful for the lovely things in life and character that I see in others. Let my eyes be open to recognize the pure gold of your Kingdom.

You tell me to put God first in everything, to love him with all my heart and mind and will. Let me put no other person before you, but love you first and foremost, so that I may love others with your love. Let me put no object before you or make any idol which shall usurp the place in my heart which only you have the right to occupy. Let no desire or ambition take the place in my valuation and affection which only your wise, good and loving will should occupy.

O Christ, my Lord, I hardly dare ask what it is I still lack before I can have your quality of life, for I know that you will unerringly put your finger on the thing I value most, the thing I am most reluctant to let go. Only if I will sell all that I have, paying the last farthing, will I get the treasure of your Kingdom, your rule in my life, and so be completely free to be what you want me to be, to do what you want done and bear all that you allow to happen to me, so that everything may work together for good, for sanctification, for blessing.

Matthew 6:19–21, 13:44–45; Mark 10:17–22, 12:28–34

16. Rejecting Anxiety

Philippians 4:11. *I have learned to be content, whatever the circumstances may be.* (J.B.P.)

O Christ, my Lord, you tell me that anxiety springs from a divided loyalty: I try to serve two masters – you and the worldly spirit. You teach me that anxiety is a subtle sin, amounting to distrust of God's goodness and his intention for his children.

You point to the birds in their myriads, who find enough food provided by nature, and you tell me that people are of much more value to you than birds. You tell me also that not a sparrow falls without your knowledge and compassion. It is true, O Lord, that most of us want and eat much more than we need to keep us alive and healthy, that some of us have to take indigestion tablets to counteract our over-eating.

We think we must have enough changes of clothes to keep up with our neighbours or with changing fashions, and you tell us of the simple beauty of wild flowers, more beautiful than a king in his royal robes or a Bishop in his cope and mitre.

You warn us that anxiety is not only sinful but foolish, for in itself it can change nothing, but only make us divided and muddled, so that we cannot think clearly or act decisively.

Put God's Kingdom first, you say, and everything needed to implement it will come as a bonus. Don't let worries about tomorrow spoil us for life today, which has enough problems and duties for anyone, without worrying about things which may never happen.

Yet, dear Lord, many people die of starvation every day and many shiver in the winter cold. How am I to understand this, my Lord? Is it that your provision in nature is enough if we live wisely and unselfishly? Is there enough for everyone's need, but not for everyone's greed? If all cared for each and each for all, would there be enough?

Does the Church teach the world your values and principles as you taught those first twelve Christians? Does it put people first or its own life? Does it make people feel uncomfortable with words as challenging as yours? Does the Church act as the conscience of people, nagging away until something is done?

O Christ, my Lord, it is a complex world, in which the individual can do so little, once things go wrong. But you are at work in it, you know the kind of world you want, which is the same that ordinary people want – a world at peace, free from fear, free from want, with healthy bodies, happy homes, and contented minds.

You call me to help you get that world. I will try to be simply loyal to you, to love and care for my neighbours near or far, and to stand for the values of your Kingdom. Teach me how to make right judgements, to make courageous decisions, show me how to live, and make me an active unit of love in your computer of divine intention.

Matthew 6:24–34; Philippians 4:6–7, 10–13; James 1:2–7

17. Humble Service

Galatians 5:13. *Through love be servants of one another.* (R.S.V.)

O Christ, my Lord, I often think of you washing the feet of your first disciples on that last night, not only teaching them the lesson of humble service, but wanting to do something personal and loving for each. I picture you kneeling at the feet of each, looking up into his eyes, remembering in a flash the story of your relationship from the first meeting with him. You knew the weakness and strength of each, his potential for the Kingdom, and what he still lacked.

It has taken quite a time, dear Lord, for me to realize that I must let you serve me before I can serve you and others. I am like Peter and want to protest that things are the wrong way round and that I should be kneeling at your feet. You warn me that unless I let you minister to me first, I shall not minister to others in the right spirit.

Often in your Kingdom, dear Lord, things have to be turned upside down. In your valuation the greatest is the one who in his own assessment is the least of all. I can see the awful temptation in this that I should still want to be the greatest and make humble service the means of becoming so.

In many places feet-washing has become a regular ritual in our remembrance of your Passion. Don't let me play a part in this, but let me lovingly, secretly, seek out those whose poor, injured, soiled feet need washing. Let me look up in love into their eyes, let my heart be warm and my hands be gentle. Perhaps my tears should drop in compassion on to their feet, in gratitude to your promise that whatever I do for the least of your brethren is somehow transfigured into doing it for you. So there are three loving hearts – mine . . . his . . . and your sacred heart.

O Christ, my Lord, you warn me that when I have done everything, I have not done very much. I am still an unprofitable servant, for at the best I have only done what you commanded me, what I owe to you. Yet, Lord, I glimpse something of what you are saying to me, something of what you are constantly doing for me. Teach me to serve you more faithfully, to give without grudging the cost, to continue in moments of warm devotion or times of cold duty, so that from time to time others may be drawn into the arms outspread on the cross, into the embrace of the eternal love.

John 13:1–16; Luke 22:24–27, 17:7–10; Galatians 5:13; Philippians 2:5–8

18. The Resistance of Love

Romans 12:21. *Do not let evil conquer you, but use good to defeat evil.* (N.E.B.)

O Christ, my Lord, you held before your trainees a very high standard, the goal of God's perfection of love for all. Justice is not enough in your Kingdom, however much it may have been an advance in the days of unlimited revenge. We are not to hit back with fist or word when attacked; there must be a resistance of love, which does not acquiesce in the other's evil but will not participate in deserved retaliation.

We must disarm our aggressive and even defensive instincts, and be ready to accept a further blow. When people steal from us we must be ready to let them have more than they have taken. When compelled by force or authority to do some service, we must add a further contribution of free and willing service, giving more than is required.

You tell us to love our enemies and so to turn them into friends. You tell us to pray for those who hurt us, so that we can have no resentment against them. I can see, O Lord, that this is the way to banish hostility from my heart, you hint that it will win the other man.

I am to give to anyone who wants something from me, not always what he wants but what will help him. There must be nothing but love in my heart, if I am to be with you a true child of God.

O Christ, my Lord, you put into practice what you taught those first trainees. In the guard room, crowned with thorns and wearing an old purple cloak, with your face red from the blows of scorn and the blood from the thorns, and with the spittle of the soldiers, you did not fail in love. When the nails were driven into your hands and feet, you found excuse for those who had brought you to that point, you prayed for them.

My Lord, I will need a lot of discipline and training. I hit back so quickly, perhaps not with blows, but with aggressive or defensive words. Help me to remember your teaching and example, and give me true love so that I am not self-righteous or only dutiful, but patient, loving and compassionate, seeking to understand, not acquiescing in the aggression, not self-pitying or defeated, but resisting with invincible love – as you did, as God, your Father and my Father, eternally does.

Matthew 5:38–48; Romans 12:17–21; Ephesians 4:25–32; 1 Peter 2:21–23

19. Teacher

John 3:2. *Rabbi, we know that you are a teacher come from God.* (R.S.V.)

O Christ, my Lord, your first hearers were impressed by the note of authority in your teachings; they observed that you did not teach like a professional scribe, constantly quoting the thoughts and sayings of others, but you spoke as if you had authentic experience of God. They came in crowds to listen to your teaching, to enjoy the freshness and wit of the stories you told. Many people in Nazareth wondered at 'the gracious words' you spoke, though others were offended. An uncommitted yet interested Pharisee could say, 'We know you are a teacher come from God,' and give you the title of Rabbi, though he and others knew that you had not been trained in a rabbinical theological school.

Your teaching, dear Lord, was simple and direct, relevant to people's lives and experience, yet requiring attention and thought before its deeper meaning became clear. You did not hesitate to exaggerate in order to make your point, as when you spoke of a camel going through the eye of a needle, or the Kingdom being like the smallest known seed, or of the completely impossible debt that the unmerciful servant owed his master which would take a lifetime to repay.

You often put together stories from nature or common life or from your observance of people's behaviour which arrested your hearers by their vividness or strangeness or wit, yet leaving sufficient doubt about the precise application to encourage people to tease out the meaning.

Your first disciples were intrigued about your frequent use of parables, and you emphasized how blessed they were to be enabled by you to see the point of each. Others were not so quick to understand, or to have the privilege of having an intimate relationship with you in which they could ask for further explanation. In your wisdom and compassion you told them unforgettable stories, whose point they might not immediately see, but which they would remember until one day the point would become clear.

O Master, I cannot accept Matthew's interpretation that parables were meant to disguise the meaning, blind the mind or harden the heart. It would be completely unlike you deliberately to veil the truth. You spoke in parables to enable the truth to enter through lowly doors.

Your parables ask for decision and action – 'Go and do likewise' – urging a Godward disposition and spiritual understanding. They have attracted people in every generation since you told them and will continue to do so. Once heard, the parables of the Good Samaritan, the Lost Sheep, the Prodigal Son and many others cannot be forgotten.

Dear Master, let me be a good pupil in your school of love and holiness, both as I study the earliest memories and faith of your first disciples, and as I listen to you and talk with you, the Everliving One.

Mark 1:21–22; Luke 4:22; Matthew 7:28–29, 7:24–25; Mark 4:33–34; Matthew 13:10–16; John 3:1–2

20. Disciple and Master

John 15:5. *Whoever remains in me, with me in him, bears fruit in plenty.* (J.B.)

O Christ, my Lord, you tell me that I am to be as closely in relation to you as the branch to the vine, so that your life flows into me. There is to be a mutual indwelling, 'Abide in me and I in you,' so that instinctively I begin to think like you, see what you want done and the spirit in which it is to be carried out. Then the fruit comes almost spontaneously; I don't have to plan it, or strive for it, but let you provide it.

Lord, you tell your disciples to judge others by the fruits produced. I recognize that others will judge us in the same way. If they see in our lives love, joy, peace, perseverance, kindness, goodness, faithfulness, gentleness and self-control, they will recognize that your Spirit is at work within. Our intimate relationship with you will generate these lovely products of discipleship, not to be striven for one by one, but all growing spontaneously and progressively, like the growth and ripening of fruit on a good tree.

Dear Master, in one way I am different to the branch on the vine: I can stay in the spiritual vine or cut myself off from it. Then you warn me that I am no longer any good for your grapes, but just shrivel up and die. Lord, I find that when I have stayed with you for some time, if I become self-sufficient I have no sparkle or resourcefulness. Keep me united to you.

When I remain continuously with you, I seem to acquire something of your mind, your outlook and attitude to people and happenings. Grant that I may look at people through your eyes, and see their needs and their potential for the Kingdom. Help me to see God at work within all that happens, to turn it to the furtherance of his wise and loving will.

There are many things happening in the world, dear Lord, which are clearly not the Father's will, in which I see no way of influencing for good. Perhaps my prayers will, in some mysterious working of divine providence, keep such situations tied to you, not let you get pushed out. Perhaps, Lord, there is a network of human solidarity, a kind of collective relationship in which both good and evil impulses can be transmitted. Or maybe each loving disciple is a little lump of divine yeast to help leaven the whole, or a sprinkle of salt or a little candle of light.

Dear Lord, I want to stay with you, and if possible be useful to you.

John 15:1-8; Galatians 2:20, 5:22-23; 2 Corinthians 5:16-18; John 17:24; Matthew 18:20; Acts 18:9-10; Revelation 22:1-2

21. The Same Training

Luke 6:40. *The disciple is not superior to his teacher; the fully trained disciple will always be like his teacher.* (J.B.)

O Christ, my Lord, you often had to rebuke your first disciples for lack of understanding and slowness of heart. I imagine that you often dealt with each one personally and privately, perhaps as you journeyed through the countryside or sat under the stars at night.

I picture you at the feet-washing in the Upper Room, coming to each in turn and looking up into his eyes, recalling the whole story of his discipleship, seeing his potential and what still needed to be set right, grateful for his loyalty, but longing to bring him to your own maturity. Do you kneel at my feet, O Master and Lord, and desire to do something similar for me?

I seem to see in your relationship with Peter a pattern for your dealing with each individual disciple, welcoming courageous impulses of faith yet sadly aware of the lack of stability to follow them up, as when in a moment of mounting hostility he declared faith in you as the Christ and a few moments later resisted your conviction of suffering ahead. Or on the stormy lake when he got out of the boat to walk to you, and then lost trust at the sight of the waves.

I seem to see in him, dear Lord, a desire to tell you what to do, almost to manage you. Lord, you must have loved him for his attempt to rescue you in the garden, though it showed a failure to understand the defencelessness of love. Yet it drew from you that amazing warning that all who take the sword will inevitably invite retaliation.

I have a feeling, O Master, that he was no coward, but he was offended, hurt and critical, which resulted in repudiation when challenged, yet one look from you as you were led across the courtyard could melt his burning heart and send him out into the darkness to weep his penitence, and so be ready for your forgiveness. I run with him to the tomb on the resurrection morning, anxious for your dead body, and later on that great day experience your risen presence. Dear Lord, may any failure of faith, any subtle denial that I belong to you, bring me with him to loving penitence and reinforce the desire of my heart to be your man still in whatever happens.

Most of all, dear Master, I listen with a trembling heart to your threefold question, 'Do you really love me?', with its gentle, critical reproach . . . and its implicit assurance of forgiveness, its repeated acceptance of discipleship and commission to care for all who follow you. Dear Lord, I answer with Peter, 'You know that I love you!' and I pray for grace like him to make this true.

Lord, you deal with me as sharply as you did with Peter and perhaps as hopefully, so that becoming firm in faith in you and humbly, gratefully loving in heart, I may reach that maturity of spirit which your other great disciple saw as the goal of each follower, that I may come near to the fullness of your own perfect maturity and spiritual stature. Lord, help me to press on with eager expectation to know you, share in your travail for the souls of all, becoming growingly like you and attain with you the full and eternal resurrection life.

Peter: John 1:40–42; Luke 5:8–11; Matthew 14:31; Mark 8:29, 32–33; Luke 22:31–34; John 18:10–11; Luke 23:54–62; John 21:15–19
James and John: Mark 1:19–20, 3:17; Luke 9:51–56; Mark 10:35–45
Paul: Ephesians 3:14–19; Philippians 3:8–11

PART IV

Praying

22. The Master at Prayer

John 11:41. *Father, I thank you for hearing my prayer. I knew indeed that you always hear me.* (J.B.)

O Christ, my Lord, how fortunate and blessed your first disciples were to see you at prayer and often to hear the prayers you offered to the Father. At every new development you went to him to discover its significance and to find out his will in it.[1]

At the tomb of Lazarus you expressed your confidence that the Father always heard your prayer, telling us of the power of God that always came in response.[2]

On that last night you prayed the great priestly prayer for your disciples that they should be kept in truth, guarded against evil, united in love, filled with joy and kept in union with the Father and yourself. O dear Lord, you prayed this great prayer not only for them but for all who should come to God through them, for each and all of us today, and for each succeeding generation of disciples.[3]

So I know, O Lord, that you are still praying for us as you told Peter when you warned him that he would be offended. There are times, O Lord, when I do not understand your action in me or for me. Keep me trusting and faithful, knowing that each experience may make me more mature and holy, so that I in time can help you to strengthen the brethren, yours and mine.

Lord, I am grateful that one of the three who tried to watch with you in Gethsemane was awake enough to hear

1. Luke 3:21; Mark 1:35; John 6:15; Luke 6:12–13, 10:21–22
2. John 11:41–42
3. John 17

the agonizing cry as you faced the certainty of death and sweated blood, ending with the acceptance of the Father's will that you should go forward to the cross, trusting him to accomplish the divine purpose of love. Strengthen me, O Christ, by the memory of Gethsemane and Calvary to go forward in faith in all that I may be called to experience, in pain of body or tension of spirit.[4]

O dear Lord, I marvel at the first word from the cross when you prayed for forgiveness for all who had any part in bringing you there, excusing them for their ignorance. I listen with grieving heart to these prayers from the cross, standing with Mary and John, and hearing that great cry of pain and faith when even the Father seemed hidden, yet you still called 'My God, my God!' And I rejoice in the peace of the last cry when you commended your spirit into the hands of the Father.[5]

Dear Lord, I want to pray like you – in faith, in love, in complete trust in the Father, at every step in life, and when the moment comes for me to move over the horizon into your Kingdom of the spirit.

4. Mark 14:32–36
5. Luke 23:34; Mark 15:34; Luke 23:46

23. The Model Prayer

Matthew 6:9. *This is how you should pray.* (N.E.B.)

O Christ, my Lord, I imagine that you must have prayed in this way very often yourself. The first two words express for us the close relationship between you and God and remind us of the phrase you used so often when you spoke of God as 'my Father and your Father'. We do indeed come to God as Father through you; without you we would not have dared to speak to him in this intimate way.

I come to God with you, O Lord, and I come with and on behalf of all my fellow men, a tiny representative of the whole human race, which is his family.

I notice, dear Lord, that you ask me to pray for God first of all – his name and reputation, his Kingdom of righteousness and love, his will so good, so loving, so wise, his long-term purpose for the universe and his immediate detail in our daily lives.

Then you ask us to pray for the things we need to enable us to fulfil these prayers for the great things of God. We need food for body and spirit, we need forgiveness for our sins and the ways in which we fall short of God's glory and will for us, we need to be alerted to the forces of evil, within and without, and we need divine protection in trial and temptation.

You tell us to pray for food for today, one day at a time, not looking too far ahead, but asking God's provision for the immediate present, and trusting him for the future. Dear Lord, I am conscious of the hungry millions in the world today, who in a world of plenty are in poverty and want. Help us to help them in every possible way, and goad us by your Spirit until we build a new order closer to your will.

71

I know, dear Lord, that we need nourishment for the spirit as well as the body, the bread of life which nourishes us to undertake the duties and meet the happenings of each day. Give us, dear Father, this living bread day by day.

O Christ, my Lord, I can never exhaust the contents and meaning of this prayer you have given us. Let me never say it thoughtlessly or just as a duty, but as the living touch with the God and Father of us all, as his loving, grateful, obedient children, growing up in your likeness, with your mind and your love. Glory be to God for ever, glory to you, O Christ, my Brother, for taking me to him, the Eternal Father of us all.

Matthew 6:9–13; Luke 11:1–4

24. A Place of Quiet

Psalm 62:1. *For God alone my soul waits in silence.*
(R.S.V.)

O Christ, my Lord, you often went apart to be quiet with the
Father, in the desert near Jericho, in the hills of Galilee, on
the slopes of the Mount of Olives, in the Garden of Gethsemane, in the pressure of people's needs, in the criticism
and opposition of the religious leaders, in the suspicion of
the civil authorities. You needed the refreshment of being
in the Father's presence, his insight into the meaning of the
things that were happening, his guidance when decisions
were needed, and always his love to warm and strengthen
the heart.

You told your first followers that they should go into their
own room, shut the door and pray to the Father in secret.
I think, dear Lord, you meant the chamber of the heart,
where I can be alone with the Father, just fixing all my
attention on him, lifting up my heart in love, dependence
and worship.

You tell me that the Father does not want a lot of speaking from me, though there are times when I pour out my
heart to him in anxiety, bitterness or even exultation. So I
learn the value of silence when even the machinery of
thought needs to run down and stop, and I reach a stillness
of mind, a sound of gentle stillness like the rustle of a
summer breeze through the ripening corn or the murmur
of the sea in the distance.

It is in that stillness, Lord, that you can speak, for my
heart is ready and the inner ear is alert and listening. Speak,
Lord, for your servant is listening. Sometimes there is no
voiced word from you but only the loving intercourse with
the Father, when I realize his constant presence with me.

73

Is this prayer of quiet the way in which you give us your peace? – as you promised those first disciples when their hearts were troubled, in your warnings of suffering ahead: 'Peace I leave with you, my peace I give unto you, not as the world gives,' but a peace which passes all understanding.

You remind me of the seed's need of quiet growth in the soil before it can germinate and grow into a plant for food or a flower for beauty, and I learn that the seed of the divine Word within me needs time to make itself heard and to relate itself to my life.

There are other times, dear Lord, when I am in the presence of disaster or widespread suffering, when I can only remain silent in perplexed sympathy, yet knowing that the Father's will is good and loving and that he is always working to turn pain and seeming evil into good. At such times, dear Lord, I can trust, though I may not understand or be able to justify to others, the Father's providence.

I learn also, dear Lord, availability in silence when I stand in your presence available for you to use, if I can be of use to you or to your other children, like Mary of Nazareth when she said, 'Behold the handmaid of the Lord, be it unto me according to your word,' or as your prophet Isaiah who, in a moment of vision when a messenger was needed, cried out, 'Here am I, send me.'

Train me, dear Lord, in the inmost chamber of the heart to be still and quiet, listening and expectant, in quiet trust and deepening love.

Matthew 6:5–6; 1 Kings 19:9–13; Psalm 46:10; John 14:27; Luke 1:38; Isaiah 6:9

25. In His Name

Psalm 130:5. *I wait for the Lord, my soul waits, and in his word I hope.* (R.S.V.)

O Christ, my Lord, I learn from you that the object of prayer is not just to get from God the things we want or think we need, but to get to know God in actual experience and living truth – not just to know about him. You tell me that this is eternal life, the most valuable and satisfying thing, which admits us into eternity now and prepares us for life hereafter. To know the Creator, to be able to speak to him in the homely word *Abba* which you must have used so often in the home at Nazareth, to be conscious of his presence wherever I am and whatever happens to me, to be conscious that his everlasting arms are always around me and beneath me and that nothing can seize me out of his hand. What assurance and joy this gives to the heart! And when I need to know more about him all I have to do is to look at your life and to listen to your words which your earliest disciples treasured up, even though they had to speak in the thought forms of their own day, with their interpretation of the world about them.

Yet I learn from you, dear Lord, that I may ask the Father for what I need, knowing that he is concerned about those needs. I know that my secret life is not hid from him and that my inmost heart is open before him and all my desires known.

I learn from you that one aim in my prayer must be to discover his will, his great loving will for humanity and his will for me both in my inner being and in my daily behaviour, and how to receive from him the grace and power to co-operate with him. I know that his grace will be sufficient for me and that in everything that happens I need never be defeated, but that the greater the need the more abounding the grace.

I know, dear Master, that I can bring others to the Father in prayer, both those whom I love and those who need comfort and supporting grace. O Lord, I do not know how prayer acts, but through you I believe that my concern and prayer can be a channel for your love, and that I should offer myself to help him to help them in any way possible.

Lord, there are dreadful happenings in the world, causing widespread suffering, which seem almost impossible to explain or do anything about. Perhaps my prayer can help to keep those situations tied to God, so that he is not pushed out, however grievous the circumstances or recalcitrant the people involved in them.

And, dear Lord, I am learning in this touch with you and the Father, that grace is at work within me, making me more holy and loving, more dependent and grateful, more expectant and alert, confident that the Father is always working for the welfare of his creation and the growth in maturity of every one of his children. O Lord, continue, I pray you, to teach me to pray and to assure me that prayer as you have taught it to me is the most important activity in which I ever engage.

John 17:3, 4:31–34, 11:1–3, 14:13, 15:7; Philippians 4:6

PART V
Healing

26. The Healer

Acts 10:38. *He went about doing good and healing all that were oppressed by the devil, for God was with him.* (R.S.V.)

O Christ, my Lord, those who first met you and observed you in your contacts with the sick, the suffering and the needy were struck by your compassion. In our age, dear Lord, we know so much more about widespread suffering and want: grant us your compassionate and loving heart, and a desire to heal the sufferings of people, those whom we know personally and the millions more about whom we hear.

I see, dear Lord, a great increase in compassion, through your Church and through the welfare services of nations working together, and through health services, through quick readiness to help in sudden emergencies, and through measures to provide sufficient food to keep people in health and strength. With you, O Master, I thank our Father that he is so constantly and magnificently at work. It is as if the whole world is learning the divine compassion which animated you.

O dear Lord, you emphasized the need of faith, you almost said that there could not be healing without faith, not that your healing power would be withdrawn, but that it could only operate if people opened themselves to its operation. I have the feeling, O Master, that you were pointing to the amazing self-recovery service in the human body, and were urging us to co-operate with it, with trust and gratitude.

It looks as if you were helping people to faith in the loving God whom you dared to represent. You did so much to help the suffering individual by your touch – unveiling

79

the eyes of the blind, touching the tongue of the dumb, putting your fingers into the ears of the deaf, laying loving hands on many as if sharing your strength and desire to help.

Lord, you did not limit your healing to your own people: you healed the servant of the Roman centurion and the daughter of the Syrian woman, and you reminded your hearers of earlier cures and care, as with Naaman and the Zarephath widow. Dear Lord, I have learned of the great compassion of the Buddha, and of the prophet Muhammad's constant reference to God as both compassionate and compassioning.

Dear Master, governments have taken over much of the physical healing that your Church pioneered as an agency of your love. I thank our Father for this, for I see that it releases your followers to minister to needs so far not met, and to work to preserve the loving personal caring which you showed us, so that all may consider the heart of love and the will to victorious life, which you have taught us to see embedded in the universe and sown in the hearts of people everywhere and in every generation.

The Master's Compassion: Mark 1:41, 5:19, 8:2; Matthew 9:36, 14:13–14; Luke 7:13

Extensive Healing: Mark 1:32–34; Matthew 4:23, 9:35

Emphasis in Parables: Luke 10:33, 36–37; Matthew 18:33

Necessity and Efficacy of Faith: Mark 2:5, 6:5, 5:34, 10:52, 9:23–24; Luke 8:48, 17:19

Command to Heal: Matthew 10:8; James 5:14–15

Healing available for all: Matthew 8:1–7, 15:28; Luke 5:25–27

27. Personality Diseases

Jeremiah 17:14. *Heal me, O Lord, and I shall be healed; save me, and I shall be saved.*   (A.V.)

O Christ, my Lord, I learn from you how wrong attitudes and inner inhibitions can lead to physical defects. With the paralysed man in Capernaum brought to you by four faithful friends who refused to be put off by difficulties, I see how you perceived his real trouble, a haunting sense of guilt which could not accept forgiveness. You looked into his eyes and heart and spoke the healing word he needed, 'Son, your sins are forgiven.' In the spiritual authority with which you spoke he was ready for further obedience: 'Take up your bed and walk!' – and to everyone's astonishment he flexed the muscles so long unused, and in that response of faith, body was healed as well as spirit.

O risen Lord, I see in your sending out your first disciples on that first evening of the new era, with a Gospel of forgiveness, the extension of the healing in Capernaum.

There was another man, O Lord, sick at the heart of his being, the man at the Bethesda pool, crippled by wanting to escape the responsibilities of life. You asked him a penetrating question, 'Wilt thou be made whole?' hinting that he did not really want to be healed and was unwilling to make the effort needed after years of inactivity and excuse.

Dear Lord, some of us at some time or other are in the situation of one or other of these two invalids: we can almost induce an illness to form a respectable excuse for getting out of some seemingly unpleasant duty or one of which we are afraid. Or our hangdog inner feeling of guilt paralyses us from effective living. Let me cry in desire and faith with the prophet Jeremiah, 'Heal me, O Lord, and I shall be healed; save me, and I shall be saved; for thou are my praise.'

Dear Lord, there are other diseases of spirit of which we are becoming conscious today, the feeling of being of no value which leads to value-asserting acts like compulsive stealing or extravagant spending, the fear of ridicule which makes us morbidly self-conscious or makes us retire into the dark of migraine, and sometimes wrong treatment by parents or teachers in childhood, the overburden of life which sometimes expresses itself in asthma, or faithless anxiety which results in ulcers.

Dear Lord, you were never worried or hurried or on the edge of a psychological breakdown, you were never divided in loyalty but always integrated in the wise, good, loving will of the Father. You teach us that God's grace is sufficient for us, and that to be aware of our weakness is exactly the right opportunity for your grace.

O Christ, my Lord, teach me to model my life on yours, so that I may experience the abundance of life which is the Father's will and which was the motive of your coming among us.

Mark 2:1–12 (paralysed by guilt)
John 5:1–9 (crippled by escapisms)
Luke 14:16–18 (rationalized excuses)
Luke 19:20–26 (fear of failure)

28. Restoring Control

Mark 5:9. *'What is your name?' Jesus asked.* (J.B.)

O Christ, my Lord, I can see that you were not afraid of this poor demented man, though he was probably afraid of you, for others had often caught and chained him up. I can imagine that at your approach he cried out in alarm, for living in his own subjective mind, he would be sensitive of what was going on in yours and of your wish to heal him.

You spoke in terms of the understanding of mental sickness current at the time, the belief in spirit possession. Only so could you communicate with him.

I picture you sitting quiet and silent alongside of him, letting the stillness of your mind, your compassion and love embrace him. Then you spoke with authority, commanding the violent, troubling spirit to depart.

Then you ask, 'What is your name?' recalling him to his real identity, treating him as a fellow human being, entering into personal relationship with him. He responds, 'My name is legion,' implying that he is torn by a whole host of conflicting forces.

The inner divisions are healed by a new control, the rival forces acknowledge a new authority, and the man is discovered by your disciples and local folk, sitting with you, clothed and in his right mind. Quite understandably, dear Lord, he wants to stay with you, be dependent on you, but you send him back to his home and family, assuring him of the reality of his cure and the continuing goodness of God.

Dear Lord, I find it difficult to accept the rationalized explanation of the destruction of the pigs. I cannot believe that you would destroy any of your Father's creatures. It must have been the shouting and violent actions of the man before he was healed which sent them rushing down the slope into the sea.

O Christ, my Lord, there are many poor demented people today and much seemingly senseless violence. Can it be that the sufferers have lost their identity and no longer feel in possession of themselves? Let the divine will for healing make itself known, the divine love be felt within the being of each, may the divine peace calm them, may all the inner divisions be integrated in a newly accepted Lord!

O healing representative from God, bless all who care for the sick in mind and the violent in spirit, grant them your peace of mind, your integrating unity, and your unfailing love and patience, so that the Father's will for their happiness and mature personality may be as active and effective today as it was by the shores of Galilee in the days of your physical presence!

Mark 5:1–20; 1 John 4:18

29. Opening Blind Eyes

John 9:25. *All I know is this: once I was blind, now I can see.* (N.E.B.)

O Christ, my Lord, the Scriptures of your people which you knew so well and the Scriptures about you which I study additionally, speak much about the healing of blindness and the first gift of sight.

I see that it is the Father's will that the blind should see. I have known two of your friends who devoted their lives to concern for the blind: one who taught them to overcome the handicaps of blindness in teaching them a written language of their own and training them in independence; the other who estimated that he and his colleagues must have carried out something like a hundred thousand operations for cataract. O dear Lord, I thank you for the inspiration of your love and healing care. I see in it the fulfilment of your promise that your disciples shall do greater things than you did in the short years of your physical presence with us, because you would be with the Father in his omnipresence and in his healing, saving power.

I observe, dear Master, that the continuing blind seem more sensitive in touch, more acute in hearing, more aware in intuition. And now I learn that even greater things are ahead and the blind may be enabled to see through the skin, when the eyes do not respond to healing efforts. O unique and most loving Son of the Father, I worship him for the continuance of his creating and redeeming activity.

O Christ, my Lord, I see also your emphasis on spiritual sight. I begin to see faith as a kind of in-seeing, a seeing into the spiritual dimension, glimpses of the Father always at work, understanding of the spiritual factors involved in every situation and their primacy. I begin to see how the human spirit operates, both creatively and negatively. With eyes opened by you I see so much goodness in people and I grieve over the ignorance, the wrong thinking, the sinful actions, the tragedies of human life, and the blindness that fails to see that they that are with us are more than they that are against us. Open the eyes of everyone, dear Lord, to see that nothing can separate us from the love of God which you embody and bring to our hearts. I thank you, dear Lord, for the eye-of-the-spirit which sees that there is nothing in life or death for which your grace will not be sufficient.

Help me to hold on in faith, seeing the God and Father who is invisible to the physical eye and the proud self-sufficient mind, and grant me the single eye and the purity of heart which you urge on me so that I may have the full beatitude of seeing God.

Isaiah 35:5–6, as a mark of the Messianic age, which has come in Our Lord's healing ministry, Matthew 11:4–5.
Mark 8:22–26 and 10:46–52 record two cures of blindness, and John 9 is a whole chapter dealing with a sight-giving sign.
Psalm 119:18 prays for spiritual sight.
2 Kings 6:11–17 shows a prophet's power of spiritual sight.
Matthew 5:8 and Hebrews 11:27 speak of the greatest and final blessing.

30. Love of Children

2 Kings 4:26. *Is it well with the child?* (A.V.)

O Christ, my Lord, you must have got your understanding and love of children from the children of Nazareth. I picture children loving the stories you told of farmers, women in the home, shepherds and lost sheep, parents and runaway sons, kings and their servants, told in such vivid detail, with so many human touches and flashes of humour. Perhaps later you remembered the stories told to the Nazareth children and used them on your countrywide journeys.

No wonder people brought their children to you to be touched by your healing and blessing hands, confident that you would respond to their urgent appeals. Dear Lord, many people today are deeply troubled by the sufferings of children. Lord, once at what I thought was your bidding I worked in a children's hospital and saw many joyful examples of healing, but also troubling examples of congenital cancer, disease and mental trouble. Your healings of children assure me of the Father's will for health and healing.

Your will to heal has inspired your followers all down the generations, to care for the sick and especially the children, until today healing and prevention are priorities in every nation.

I can imagine your gratitude to skilled doctors, caring nurses, persistent research workers, dutiful auxiliaries, warmhearted organizers, health visitors, as they take part in God's ministry of health. Keep your love active in their hearts and hands.

Lord, I am bothered by the knowledge of brain damage and disablement among children. The Father's heart must be broken by the knowledge of it all. I can only believe that he is always at work. I see the progressive conquest of disease – smallpox, malaria, malnutrition – and I know that one day there will be cures and prevention for things that at present we think of as incurable.

Lord, I know that love is the greatest of all healing medicines. I think of a home in Nazareth today where mentally retarded children are being saved, not just by psychological insight and skill, but even more by loving personal care and near-divine valuation of the dearness of each.

O dear Master, there are new mysteries to solve, battered babies, neglected children, many wrongly treated in childhood, spoiled for later living, many unloved, and so unable to love in return.

Lord, I cannot produce an explanation which will satisfy myself or others. I can only trust the Father's love revealed by you. In the thought of that imperative of trust, I remember one of the Father's prophets and ask as he did, 'Is it well with the child?', and hear the quiet reply from the heart of the Father, 'It is well!'

Mark 10:13–16 shows Christ's love of children, and his demand for a childlike spirit of simplicity, trust and wonder.
Mark 9:42 speaks of the dreadfulness of causing little ones to stumble.
Matthew 18:10 warns us not to undervalue children.
Mark 5:21–34, 7:24–30, 9:14–29 speak of healing children.
Luke 19:41–44 and 23:27–28 show his realization of the suffering of children in war. His knowledge of the Bible of his people would have included the vision of Zechariah 8:4–5 of Jerusalem at peace, with children playing happily in the streets and people living to a ripe old age.

31. Why Could Not We?

Matthew 17:20. *Your faith is too small.*   (N.E.B.)

O Christ, my Lord, your disciples today are as helpless as your earliest ones on the slopes of Mount Tabor, with the distraught father and the epileptic son. We ask you the same despairing question that they did, 'Why cannot we heal as you did?' Lord, we long to do so, especially for suffering children, for children born with some defect, for mentally retarded children.

Your words to the father suggest that he did not have sufficient faith: his words to you show his desire to have that faith and his realization that only through you could he gain the necessary faith. I cry out with him, 'Lord, I believe, help thou my unbelief.'

Perhaps I do not have the measure of your compassion, perhaps I am not ready to take the same amount of trouble, but expect instant healing of sensational miracle, or expect the prayer of a few seconds, spasmodically repeated, to achieve the healing. You replied to the troubled question of your disciples: 'This kind cannot be driven out by anything except prayer.' Lord, teach me costly, continuing prayer, importunate but trusting, because the Father loves to give good gifts to his children.

Perhaps my thoughts are too much on myself, wanting the satisfaction of being a healer or the reputation or admiration which would follow.

O dear Lord, your great apostle Paul spoke of healing as a gift and added that there were differing gifts. I would love to heal, O Master. Perhaps my part is like yours, to increase people's faith, the faith of the sufferers themselves or of the parents and friends of suffering children. Perhaps I am meant to arouse sufficient faith, to activate the healing process and to help people live so maturely and wisely that they do not suffer from a sick spirit or a disordered mind.

Several of your healing acts were done at a distance, O Lord – the centurion's servant and the daughter of the Syrian woman. Do these healings suggest the efficacy of prayer? Perhaps I haven't sufficient faith and commitment to touch sick people in love.

Yet you sent your disciples out to heal, so you must mean us to do so. Perhaps I have to wait for actual situations, like Peter and John with the begging cripple at the gate of the Temple. Do I accept hopeless situations too readily and not bring you into them?

I know, dear Lord, that God's will is perfectly good and loving, that you could not and would not have healed had not this been so. Make me ready and eager to co-operate with his loving will for each.

Lord, give me a believing mind, give me a loving heart, give me blessing hands, give me trusting prayers. And thank you for the amazing amount of healing that takes place – the natural healing of the wisdom implanted by God in the body, and the healing that takes place every day in clinics, hospitals, operation theatres, research laboratories. Yet, dear healing Master, the question still nags on in my mind: 'Why cannot I?'

Mark 9:14–29

32. Unanswered Question

Revelation 7:17. *God shall wipe away all tears from their eyes.* (A.V.)

O Christ, my Lord, in every age people have been troubled by the mystery of suffering. Sometimes many think that all suffering is inflicted by God and therefore those who try to be God-fearing should be exempt. Lord, I am not sure if Job was a historical character or whether his wrestling with the problem was in the mind of the writer of that human drama. I see both the faith of Job and of the writer in the words 'Though he slay me yet will I trust in him'. I am more grateful for the peace of mind and heart which he found in his touch with the Father and the experience of hearing God and in some way seeing him, which made him ready to live trustingly with the problem unexplained.[1]

Lord, there was that earlier Servant of the Lord whom you studied so deeply, who suffered for his people and was finally done to death, whom some believed won forgiveness for others by his innocent suffering. Your followers in every age have seen in him a model of your saving activity, your identification with sinful people and your readiness to face death, trusting in the Father to make your obedience effective for others.[2]

Dear Lord, you did not solve the problem in a way which would enable me to convince by argument the many people troubled by actual suffering or the burden of the problem. But you bore on your heart their troubles, you healed many suffering people and so showed us that suffering was not the direct will of God, but that he is always working to

1. Job 13:15, 42:1–6
2. Isaiah 52:13–53:12

heal. Lord, I am deeply grateful for your assurance that suffering is an opportunity for the will of God to be manifest and for the healing that followed this assurance.[3]

You do not solve all our troubled questions about suffering, but you teach us how to deal with suffering. I learn from you, dear Lord, not to resent it, not to allow it to knock me out, not to give way to self-pity, but to accept it as something which our God and Father did not inflict but something in which he is always working to bring a greater blessing than if the unhappy thing had never happened. Deepen, O Master, this faith in me, enlarge my heart to the measure of your compassion, and arouse faith in all sufferers in the eternal goodness of God which will not allow any conceivable trouble to separate us from his love so active in you. You teach us, dear Lord, that in all that happens we can be more than conquerors through the love and grace of the Father, which you came to make available.[4]

Lord, many people bring suffering on their own heads by wrong living or by foolish, unrighteous acts. Let the loving forgiveness of God help them to a new way of life. There are other things which people suffer because of our human solidarity, either through infection or mistake or the free action of others. Grant, O Lord, that we may all work to discover the cause of diseases which we call incurable and avoid disasters where human prevention is at fault.

Dear Lord, like many others, I am most troubled by the sufferings of children and the operation of heredity. Here, my Master, I can only trust the willed purpose of the Father and hope and believe that every little scrap of humanity is valued by him and gathered into his love.

3. John 9:1–3
4. Romans 8:28, 37–39; Revelation 7:17

33. In our Hands

Mark 6:38. '*How many loaves have you?*' *he asked.*
'*Go and see.*' (J.B.)

O Christ, my Lord, I have often wondered about your response to your first disciples about the hungry crowd, 'You give them something to eat.' It seems to suggest that they had some resources which could be contributed or organized. You commanded them to bring what they had to you for you to bless and use. In the end all were fed and there was plenty left over.

Lord, we your disciples today are told that one-third of the people in the world do not get enough food to eat, nor enough to keep them in health and strength, free from disease and strong enough to work to produce sufficient food.

Lord, there seems plenty of available land, there is the potential in the seed and the fertility of the soil. We have the expert knowledge to be shared, the transport available for quick supply, the central organization to deal with crop disease, locusts, erosion and irrigation. Lord, there are wealthy nations with more than enough, many of whose people have to take digestion tablets to counter over-eating and drinking, while in developing nations thousands die of hunger or disease before they have a chance of enjoying the abundant life which is the Father's will, now possible in the resources of knowledge, skill and organization available to us.

Dear Lord, if we humans live in your way, there is enough, enough to satisfy everyone's need, though not everyone's greed. I thank you that the churches are working together to bring aid to all in need, but the task is too great for individuals or generous groups to accomplish. Governments and nations alone are capable of doing this. Nations must be willing and ready for comparatively small sacrifices and governments will then feel safe and free to work together for humanity. Is it here, dear Lord, that your insight to disciples that they are to be like yeast, small active constituents in the main lump, is relevant?

It seems that the understanding of citizenship, not only within nations, but in a sense of being world citizens, is the key to meeting the world need. Dear Lord of the Kingdom, I seem to see three citizenships – each within his or her own nation, in the growth towards human unity, and in our citizenship of the Kingdom of heaven which must govern the other two citizenships.

Lord, we have to rid our hearts of selfishness, and work together to socialize the golden rule to love our neighbour as ourselves. The world, dear Lord, is the neighbourhood and the context in which we have to exercise our discipleship today. Lord, it is in our own hands to get the world of your will. If there is failure, it will be ours not yours. But we still need your compassion, your inspiration, your constant reminder that we are our brother's and brothers' keepers, and your vision and will for abundant life for all, and above all your loving heart, beating with the eternal love.

Mark 6:30–44 – the responsibility lies on the disciples
Matthew 25:31–46 – nations will be judged
James 2:14–17 – religious profession is not enough
1 Corinthians 16:1–4 – a beginning of corporate aid
John 10:10 – the purpose of Christ's coming
Revelation 22:1–2 – God's will for health and plenty

PART VI

Encounters

34. The Faith of a Soldier

Matthew 8:10. *I have never found faith like this, even in Israel!*   (J.B.P.)

O Christ, my Lord, to a disciple who has lived in different parts of the world and has friends in many nations and in varying communities of faith, this is a heart-warming incident. You admired the faith of this Gentile soldier, for in the understanding of the chain of authority in his own profession, he saw an analogy to authority in the spiritual sphere. O Lord, how splendid it would be if everyone discovered the secret and vocation within his own context and profession, and then related it to yours. I am grateful for the memory of your boyhood when you said you must be about your Father's business, and then went back and worked for twenty years as a carpenter and builder.

You said you had not found such great faith even in Israel, which claimed to be a God-chosen community of faith. This man's faith inspired the vision of people coming from East and West to sit down in the Kingdom of God, and led you to sound a warning to all who thought they had a right to be there.

Lord, I remember the humility of this man, who in the impact of what he had learned about you felt unworthy that you should enter his home, and saw that your physical presence was not necessary for your spiritual power to operate. Grant me, dear Lord, similar humility and faith!

This Gentile had built a synagogue for the Jewish people among whom he lived. Master, occasionally your Church is led to reciprocate, for I remember when the welfare agencies of the World Council of Churches were rebuilding a Yugoslav town destroyed by earthquake they decided to rebuild the mosque as well, a recognition that there is a religious dimension in human society which needs to be provided for.

Lord, you constantly emphasized the need of faith and its efficacy, you were quick to recognize it in this man, anxious about his son, and in a Syrian woman, desperately worried about her daughter. It looks as if human parenthood at its best is a pattern of the divine and eternal parenthood of God. Perhaps every parent is closer to the origin of all parenthood than most of us know. Grant, dear Lord, that we may all be led by you into the everlasting arms, always outstretched to embrace as dear children all who have come into being by his creative love. Dear Son of God, we all need the divine Father- and Mother-hood, and many of us have found it through you. Thanks be to you for this Gospel!

Matthew 8:5–13 with Luke 7:3–5; Mark 15:21–28; Acts 10:34–35; Revelation 7:9, 21:24–27

35. A Timid Inquirer

John 3:6. *Men can only reproduce human life, but the Holy Spirit gives new life from heaven.* (L.B.)

O Christ, my Lord, the report of your preaching in Galilee and your cures of sick people must have aroused interest in Jerusalem, and they brought a Pharisee of standing to see you, under cover of darkness. I can picture you sitting together on the flat roof of the house where you were staying, feeling the gentle evening breeze on your faces.

I think you must be talking about the Kingdom of God, for suddenly you break in with a warning that unless a man undergoes a new birth from above, he will not *see* the Kingdom of God, will not understand what it is about.

Nicodemus wonders how this can happen when a man is old and set in his ways, it is as difficult as returning to his mother's womb. You repeat your warning and enlarge it a little: it must be by water and the spirit. Perhaps that means in outward symbol and inward change, perhaps it is a demand for the penitence of John's baptism and the commitment to you – 'repentance and faith'. Only so can a man enter the Kingdom; it can only come from above, from a spiritual source.

Nicodemus still wonders how this can happen, and you point to the evening breeze of which no one can identify the source or know exactly the moment when it will blow. You reproach him for failure to see the analogy, and you show your hope that an accredited teacher in Israel would have understood this.

I can picture him going away thoughtful and puzzled still. Perhaps, dear Lord, you were not too disappointed, but realized that new thinking takes time to germinate and commitment needs courage.

Yet something had happened in Nicodemus, for months later we see a result of that first meeting. In the Council, as critics and opponents plot against you, Nicodemus points out that 'our Law', which is also the Law of the Lord, provides that an accused person must be given a hearing before any sentence is passed. His colleagues scornfully suggest that he is becoming a Galilean, a follower, and assert that in the past no prophet has come from Galilee. It looks, dear Lord, as if the courage of discipleship is being born.

Your crucifixion, dear Master, brings final conviction, and Nicodemus now goes to the Governor with Joseph of Arimathaea, asks for your body, and gives it honourable burial. We do not know what sad thoughts and regrets were in their minds as they tended your body and rolled the stone to close the entry to the tomb. We are not told of their surprised joy when they heard of your continuing presence with your followers.

Dear Risen Lord, let me ponder on this experience of discipleship, give me the spiritual birth, the change of heart which took so long to happen. Let me meditate on your crucifixion and see the uttermost love expressed in it, the divine love of the Godhead, and let me surrender myself in love to be a courageous, grateful follower and a humble, faithful worker for your Kingdom.

John 3:1–13, 7:45–52, 19:38–40

36. 'She Loved Much'

Luke 7:37–38. *A woman in the city, which was a sinner, when she knew that Jesus sat at meat in the Pharisee's house, brought an alabaster box of ointment, and stood at his feet behind him weeping.* (A.V.)

O Christ, my Lord, I have often wondered about the meaning of these words of yours in their original speaking, 'a woman which was a sinner'. I have taken her to be a prostitute, making herself available for lustful or sex-starved men, perhaps for money, not keeping to one man only. Perhaps there was tenderness in her body-giving, perhaps a compassion for men in their sexual desire. You had looked into her heart, as you had looked into the eyes of many others and had seen their most characteristic feature.

Some sympathy with you had awakened a hope, a penitence, a gratitude, which called out an expression of what she now felt. You did not condone, you saw 'her sins, which are many', and you declared that they were forgiven. You saw that weighed in the balances of divine love and judgement, the weight of her love was greater than the weight of her sin.

O Lord, I remember the incident of another woman, this time caught in the very act of adultery, for which the strict legal punishment was stoning. She was accused before you, though the man involved was not. You made the accusers pause and think. With your finger you wrote something in the dust at your feet. Lord, I would like to know what you wrote: it must have been something very short and pointed. Perhaps it was connected with the words you spoke, 'Let him that is without sin cast the first stone' – sin in actual act or lust in the heart, which you spoke about in Matthew's collection of your teachings.

At any rate, the stones dropped from their hands, and one by one they went away shamefaced – 'beginning with the oldest', for the power of sex continues as long as there is life. Perhaps there is more need for forgiveness in old age than in the years of youth, when desire is so strong and so quickly recurrent.

Lord, often in married life there is more a desire for the satisfaction of sex than the mutual self-giving, the inner desire for deep union in each other. Let it be said, 'He loves much,' let love cover a multitude of sins, increase my capacity for love and decrease my impulses to throw stones, actual or mental.

Luke 7:36–50; John 8:1–11; 1 Peter 4:8; James 5:20

37. A Sympathetic Scribe

Matthew 13:52. *When, therefore, a teacher of the law has become a learner in the kingdom of heaven, he is like a householder who can produce from his store both the new and the old.* (N.E.B.)

O Christ, my Lord, I see that generally the scribes, the Biblical scholars of your day and the recorders of religious tradition, were opposed to you. I see also your diagnosis of their temptations and your stern criticism of their failings, which seem to be the temptations and failings of religious people today. I see over-scrupulosity in small details and neglect of the great principles of the divine Law. I see the danger of hypocrisy, the wearing of a mask of piety, the emphasis on outer appearance and neglect of the inmost heart. I see the temptation to fear anything new and to seek security in the past or in the conventional. I recognize the tendency to trust in rules and regulations which prevent people from entering the freedom of your Kingdom. O dear Master, let my touch with you be so intimate and deep that I become aware when these temptations get a grip on me. Strengthen me to rigorous self-examination and deliver me from evil.[1]

Yet, Lord, there were scribes who were drawn to you and open to sincerity and truth. There was the one with whom you had the discussion over the greatest commandments in the Law of the Lord, who voiced his admiring acceptance of your priorities of loving God with all one's being and one's neighbour as oneself, and your approval of his valuation. I am grateful for your tribute to him: 'You are not far

1. Matthew 23:13-28

from the Kingdom of God.'[2]

Lord, I am not sure whether he was the same scribe who wanted further definition of the meaning of personal neighbourhood, which called forth a most memorable parable.[3] I see how challengingly you changed the question from 'Who is my neighbour?' to 'Who was the true neighbour?' to the Jew lying half-killed on the Jericho road. Whether he was or not, you made it clear that true neighbourliness demands timely decision and costly action. Help me to do likewise.

Lord, it is good to know that there were some friendly interpreters of the Law handed down to your people. I remember the one who said he would follow you wherever you went, but seemingly turned back when you pointed out the cost. Lord, I am, like him, quick to protest my devotion to you, but not so ready to pay the last farthing in action and behaviour.[4]

O Christ, my Lord, I want to be a wise student of the Scriptures, of the traditions from the past, and a true interpreter of my own experience of you, bringing forth new treasures as well as preserving all that is good in the old. Let me be a disciple who has been trained by you for the Kingdom of Heaven.[5]

2. Mark 12:28–34
3. Luke 10:25–37
4. Matthew 8:19–20
5. Matthew 13:52

38. A Worried Governor

John 18:37. *For this I was born, and for this I have come into the world, to bear witness to the truth.*
(R.S.V.)

O Christ, my Lord, I marvel at the moment of judgement for both you and Pontius Pilate. I feel a lot of sympathy for him, caught between nationalist and political pressure, a fear that you might after all be a leader of revolution, a cynical understanding of your accusers, as well as the memory of earlier criticisms and reproach from his own authorities, yet underneath it all a growing feeling that you were innocent of the charge brought against you.

His direct question, 'Are you a King?' elicited the answer that your Kingdom was a kingship of truth, and that the whole purpose of your life was to witness the truth, not just the facts of the charges against you, but the truth at the heart of things, eternal truth.

In the garden you had reproved Peter for his attempt to rescue you 'by the sword', here again you made it clear that your Kingdom was of another dimension. Had it been like worldly kingdoms, you said, your servants would fight to defend and rescue you.

Lord, I have the feeling that the governor's question, 'What is truth?', was a genuine one and not a cynical jest. I can see the need for any judge to get at the truth, when he has to sift the evidence and decide the truthfulness of witnesses. I can see the desire to keep in with established authority, or in our days, public opinion. I can see also the cynical streak in Pilate when the organized crowd, in reply to his question, 'Shall I crucify your King?', shouted, 'We have no King but Caesar!'

Yet, Lord, it would seem clear that he betrayed his own

conscience, and left us a legacy of excuse when he tried to evade the responsibility of his decision by washing his hands. Save me, O Master, from doing the same. Grant that when I stand before you I may say, with a poet of your people, 'I will wash my hands in innocence, and so will I go to your altar.'

Lord, there was also the terrible shout, 'His blood be on us and on our children!', which your disciples have often held against your people as a whole, forgetting your own prayer, 'Father, forgive them for they know not what they do.'

Dear Lord, I see truth enshrined in your person, truth in the depth of the heart, truth drawn from the Father, the source of all truth. O send your light and truth into the depths of my being that I may be a witness to truth, and accompany you to the eternal brightness of the Kingdom of Truth.

John 18:28 – 19:16; Matthew 27:24–26; John 14:6, 16:13; Psalms 51:6, 43:3, 26:6–7

PART VII
Climax

39. Darkness and Glory

John 17:4–5. *I have glorified you on earth and finished the work that you gave me to do. Now, Father, it is time for you to glorify me.* (J.B.)

O Christ, my Lord, the gospels speak of darkness during your crucifixion, and your cry of desolation suggests darkness within your own spirit. At your arrest earlier you spoke of an hour under the power of darkness. On the other hand you saw your death as going to the Father, and in your great prayer for your disciples spoke of it as an hour of glory. Even when your soul was troubled in the thought of what was to happen, you did not pray to be saved from it, but only that the Father should be glorified through it. Your intimate disciples tell us that a voice came from heaven, assuring you that the Father would glorify his name as he had done before.[1]

Dear Lord, your disciples today cannot help seeing the tragedy of the cross, even though we praise God for its manifestations of unfailing love, and for the saving grace it makes available within our hearts. I remember your saying that there is no greater love than that a man should lay down his life for his friends. I remember too Paul's saying that God shows his love towards us because it was while we were still sinners and opposed to his loving will that you died for us. But I still feel the pain of your rejection and the complete injustice of your execution, the betrayal, denial and failure of your first disciples, as well as the excruciating physical pain of crucifixion.[2]

1. John 17:1–5, 12:27–28
2. John 15:13; Romans 5:8

Most of all, I feel the darkness that descended on you, when you could not feel the Father near, when only faith and love were left and you cried out that loud cry 'My God! My God!', still your God in the darkness, your faith and love piercing the cloud to the eternal love and light behind it. O dear suffering Lord, the fate of humanity trembled in the balance in that moment. This was the final deadly wound inflicted by evil, the fiercest temptation you ever experienced, the most subtle doubt, 'What if God has forsaken me?' As I look back, dearest Lord, I can't help feeling that the voice of the Father must have been saying again, 'This is my beloved Son.'[3]

Let me see also, dear Lord, the glory of the cross in that you gladly accepted the Father's will that you should continue to show his love whatever might be the reactions of men. I learn from you that there is glory when the Father's will is done as fully as possible, however difficult the circumstances.

In your cross a light has shone in the darkness, which shines down the generations until today, and will continue to shine until the end of time. O Christ, my Lord, let me take you as the light of the world, both in the uncertainties and crises of my own life, and in all the changes and confusions of the world in which I share. In all my frustrations, pain and seeming failure, let me remember the insight of another follower that you endured the cross and despised its shame for the joy that was set before you in doing the Father's will, and forwarding his purpose of love. I stand in awe and listen to that other great cry from the cross, 'It is *finished*!' Love and faith have been shown to the uttermost. Nothing more can be done, now you commit your spirit into the loving hands of the Father.[4]

Dear Master and Guide, let me follow you, the pioneer

3. Mark 15:33–34; Luke 23:44; Matthew 27:45–46
4. John 19:30; Luke 23:46

and perfecter of faith, in trusting the Father, believing that the last word is always with him, and that there will always be a third day of brightness and glory.[5]

5. Hebrews 12:1–2

40. Timeless Moment

Zechariah 3:9. *I will remove the guilt of this land in a single day.* (R.S.V.)

O Christ, my Lord, on a number of occasions you spoke of your certainty of death, almost as if it were necessary, yet with confidence that it would not be the end. In their experience of you as risen, your disciples heard your own interpretation that all that had just happened had been implicit in the Law and the Prophets and had been taken up into the Father's eternal purpose. In your meeting with Greek pilgrims you saw the rightness of accepting the cross, and when you met with your disciples on the first resurrection evening, you implied that now death had been undergone the mission to the world could begin immediately.[1]

In this firm confidence of your victory in death your first disciples saw the rightness, even the necessity of death, as well as the taking up into the eternal purpose of the Father of your suffering and death. O dear Lord, I sometimes dare to think that the cross was the real victory, and that the resurrection was the Father's seal on your sacrifice, that John was right in his vision of the redeemed in heaven and this new song celebrating the wonder of your death and its effect on every race and nation.[2]

O crucified Master, I begin to understand the symbolism of Matthew's description of the immediate consequences of your death: the veil of the Temple rent in two, showing that the way to God was now open; the very earth shaken and never being the same again; the grave no longer a prison

1. Mark 8:31, 9:12, 9:32–33; Luke 24:26–27, 44–48; John 12:20–31, 20:19–23
2. Revelation 5:9–10

but burst open and empty; risen saints streaming into the holy city, to bear their witness to the efficacy of the cross in the very place of execution and death. Later your servant Paul added another symbolic happening when he said that the dividing wall in the Temple, forbidding Gentiles to penetrate further, had been broken down by you, so that the way to the Father was open to Gentiles as well.[3] All are now the people of God, no longer strangers.

The will of the Father had been faithfully completed, O unique and beloved Son, so that in the very moment of death you could cry out in both relief and triumph, 'It is finished!' Dear Lord, I see in the moment of your death, the moment also of your resurrection, the release of your spirit to become a universalized presence, and your ascension to the Father – an eternal, timeless moment, which would take several days before its significance would dawn on your first disciples, and longer for many of your disciples today. Easter, Ascension, Pentecost are gathered into that moment of awe, when, the fullness of pain accomplished, you gave up your spirit in thankful, glorious trust to the Eternal Father.

3. Matthew 27:51–53; Ephesians 2:14

41. Love Unlimited

John 13:1. *He had always loved those who were his in the world, but now he showed how perfect his love was.* (J.B.)

Lord, as the time drew near for your death which you saw as the crown and seal of your Christhood, the disciple most conscious of your love remarked on your love for those whom you called your own, and added that you loved them to the end, to the uttermost. He realized that you were about to fulfil your own insight that there is no greater love than that a man should lay down his life for his friends, except to die for his enemies.

All through their training these first disciples had stored up your teaching and remembered your example. They had treasured your summary of the divine Law, to love God with the whole being and to love others as they loved themselves. They knew that they were even to love enemies and constantly to return good for evil. As the time for your death in love drew near, they had heard a new and final commandment, greater than the second great command, namely that they should love others as you loved them, a love without any limit or reserve.

They had seen this unlimited love in action – towards the sick and suffering, the mentally deranged, the despised tax-gatherers, the outcast lepers, the excommunicated Samaritans, non-churchgoers, sinners and harlots.

They had seen your human love for the two sisters and their brother in the home at Bethany, where you were such a welcome visitor. They had heard the message of Martha and Mary, 'Lord, he whom you love is ill,' and the comment of the spectators as you wept at the cave where he was buried, 'See, how he loved him!'[1]

Later they were to hear from John, your mother and Mary Magdalene of your last words: your prayer for forgiveness for all who had had a hand in your death, implementing your command to love enemies and to pray for those who ill-treat us; the second word assuring one (and possibly both) of the thieves of your continuing fellowship; another showing your loving provision for your mother and your trusting love in the much-loved disciple; the great cry of spiritual loneliness, still, 'My God! My God!'; and the last word in loving trust as you committed your spirit into the Father's hands.

Your love for Jerusalem was evident as you entered the city in company with the Galilean pilgrims, who knew and loved you and hoped you were the long-expected Messiah. Your sad reproach, 'Oh Jerusalem, Jerusalem!', the moving last parable of the hen gathering her chicks under her wings, and the tears as you saw the inevitable consequences of wrong policies and missed opportunities, emphasized your feelings again as you stopped for a moment to greet the women who wept at your fate. Loving Lord, many of your disciples today weep in heart if not in tears as they look over the city from the place where you wept over it, as they follow the way of the cross and stand at the traditional place where you were crucified, and weep as they remember your broken body being taken down from the cross.[2]

Dear Master, I shall never cease to marvel at the perceptiveness of your great disciples as they tried to plumb the deepest meaning of the cross. They were both led to see the love of God through it: Paul's insight that God was in you reconciling the world unto himself, more so as you were willing to die not for perfect and righteous people alone, but for sinners, rebels and drop-outs; and John's conviction, from his experience of you and long reflection in disciple-

1. John 13:1, 11:5, 3, 36
2. Luke 23:27–29; John 17:25; 1 John 3:14

ship, that God is love, together with that great gospel verse that God so loved the world that he gave you for its salvation.

Christ, dear Lord, your cross has drawn millions in every generation to you and through you to the Father. But for your cross I would not be your disciple today. The cross is the fulfilment of your prayer on the night before the cross: that all your disciples may know that the Father loves us even as he loved you, and that this divine love may be in us also.

Dearest Lord, let your love control me, enliven me, energize me, permeate mind, will and action, so that I may know that when I love, even with only a fraction of your love, I pass out of death into life, out of time into eternity, and see the source and goal of love, first glimpsed in you, the human face of God.

42. Lord, You Died Young

Isaiah 46:3–4. *Borne by me from your birth, carried from the womb; even to your old age I am He, and to grey hairs I will carry you. I have made and I will bear.* (R.S.V.)

O Christ, my Lord, sometimes I wonder what you would have shown us of God's love of men, had men not crucified you and you had lived on to old age. You would have shown us how to accept the diminishments, the failing powers, the humiliations of old age. You observed the limitations suffered by the old, as your remark to Peter by the Sea of Galilee tells us.

Even now, dear Lord, you whisper in the heart of each listening disciple what you said to Paul, 'My grace is sufficient for you, for my strength is made perfect in weakness.'

You experienced the threat and fear of death beneath the olives of Gethsemane, and when the moment came, you commended your spirit into the hands of the loving Father. You promised your first disciples that you would be preparing a place for us, that we might be with you and the Father.

Perhaps, dear Lord, the increasing weaknesses of age mean that we are being hollowed out of the physical, the material, the temporal, so that we may be filled with the spiritual and the eternal, and that our mortality may be transformed into immortality.

O Christ, my Lord, I learn from you that death is not the end of life, but the gateway into imperishable life, that it is more like birth, our final birth, with just a moment of travail and then the realization of the joy of freedom from the confining past.

You assure us that if anyone keeps your word, spoken from the heart of the Father, he will never *see* death, he will hardly notice death when it comes, but take it in his stride. You go on to promise that he will not *taste* death, he will hardly feel it, for the divine life will be so strong in him.

Lord, I cannot be as trusting as your disciple Paul when he said, 'My desire is to depart and be with Christ, for that is far better.' Help me to grow towards such trust.

O dear Master, a much later disciple said that old men should be explorers – exploring past grace in memory, exploring present grace in the depths of being, exploring the frontier ahead which they will soon cross, when we may see 'a band of angels coming after me, coming for to carry me home', where I eternally belong and where so many loved ones and old friends are waiting to welcome me.

John 21:18; Isaiah 46:3–4; Matthew 10:29–31; Isaiah 40:27–31; Luke 2:29–32; John 14:3

43. Everliving One

Revelation 1:17–18. *I am the Living One, I was dead and now I am to live for ever and ever, and I hold the keys of death and of the underworld.*
(J.B.)

O Christ, my Lord, I see from the faith of those earliest followers, that your resurrection was not just the fact that on a certain day in the early thirties of the first century a man rose from the dead, but that you are the Everliving One, ever present, everywhere present, continuously active to guide and strengthen your followers today. Exactly how this happened I cannot say, I accept the fact and its implications. It is so vital, so seminal that I can understand how people today are slow to believe and live in resurrection faith.

Sometimes I wonder if the whole of God's plan of salvation was gathered into the moment of your death – your spirit being released from its incarnation to become a universal spirit, at the same moment eternally united with the Father in an infinitely more potent way, resulting in an outpouring of love and power when the significance of that great moment was perceived.

O Risen Master, I want to live in this resurrection faith, in moments of spiritual exaltation and serene peace, and in times when faith has to be exercised, and if your presence sometimes seems hidden, the mists of doubt can be pierced by darts of love from me to you, calling forth from you infinitely more love than I can offer.

I see, dear Lord, an extra dimension of the spiritual and the eternal, and that this milieu is the real, compared with which life in this physical and temporal sphere gives but a faint indication.

Let me, O Everliving One, have resurrection life now, ever conscious of your presence, constantly seeking your interpretation of life in this world and your grace to live it trustingly and lovingly according to the principles of your gospel, and so enjoy a measure of eternal life now, a first-fruit of the final life prepared for us by the Father, attested by your life of obedience, your death in love, and your resurrection in power.

Luke 24:1–8, 24:12, 22–24, 24:25 show the gradual dawning of faith and understanding.
1 Corinthians 15:2–9 lists the witnesses; 15:12–19 stresses the vital importance for later faith; and 15:22–25 the significance for humanity.
Romans 1:1–6 emphasizes the power of God at work.
Revelation 1:17–18 crystallizes final faith.

44. Birthday Celebration

Luke 2:30–31. *Mine eyes have seen thy salvation, which thou hast prepared before the face of all people.* (A.V.)

O Christ, my Lord, I give thanks to God for your birth, every year and every day. I give thanks that you were born in poverty, so that even the poorest might feel welcome. I give thanks for Mary of Nazareth, and her readiness for God's purpose, and for Joseph's acceptance of a mystery, and for their loving care of you in the home of Nazareth.

O dear Lord, some scholars tell us that the accounts of Matthew and Luke were not historical biography, but inspired faith and interpretation. I ask myself what manner of child and man you were, that disciples should express their faith in these lovely, heart-warming stories.

Let me believe with them, that God was involved in your birth in a special way, that your birth and life were of intense interest to angels, prophets and saints. I see in the story of Bethlehem the faith of your earliest disciples that you were the spiritual successor of David, the ideal king, the fulfiller of all the hopes and intuitions of past seekers of your own people.

I see in the shepherds your availability for simple people of faith, the vast majority of our human race. And in the story of the wise men I learn that you speak to them in their own culture, history and religion, the assurance that their search will bring them to the truth of God.

I am most thankful, dear Lord, that those earliest disciples, who came to you first as teacher and master, saw that in you God had come to be with us humans in a new way, and that in your life they could learn of the heart of the Father from which you had come to make him known.

I am deeply grateful that their experience of the resurrection and their faith in you as the Everliving One led to this interpretation of your person and meaning.

In all this, dear Lord, I am your humble disciple, whatever may be the changing views about you. You come in divine mystery from God, you reveal God to me, you take me with you to God, you are always and everywhere present with me. May my faith in you make each commemoration of your coming if possible a happier birthday for you and an even deeper blessing for all who celebrate it.

Luke 1:26–38, 2:1–20; Matthew 1:18–25, 2:1–12; John 1:1–18; Galatians 4:4–7; Philippians 2:6–8

45. First Resurrection Experiences

1 Corinthians 15:20. *The glorious fact is that Christ was raised from the dead: he has become the very first to rise of all who sleep the sleep of death.*
(J.B.P.)

O Christ, my Lord, you must have chuckled on the morning of the great day when your disciples discovered that you were the Everliving One, unkilled by death, chuckled when Mary Magdalene mistook you for the gardener. I can imagine the smile in your voice as you greeted her by name: 'M-a-a-r-y.' For many years I have puzzled over your gentle reproof, 'Don't hold me!' Now at last I can see that she must not hold you to earth, that you were to be with the Father and that a new era had dawned. Mary wanted nothing more than the restoration of the old, warm human relationship, little realizing the great transformation that had taken place. So you send her to tell the glad news of what has happened and that you are with your Father and theirs, your God and theirs. You call them 'my brethren', for you are the firstborn from the dead, the first and eldest brother of all the children of God, the universal brother of all mankind.[1]

Dear Lord, I love the account of the two disciples on their walk to Emmaus, talking sadly together of the happenings of the last two days, joined by you on their journey, fulfilling the promise that when two or three are gathered together as your disciples you are present with them. I love your patient explanation that all that has happened has been taken up into the loving purpose of God, and I gasp

1. John 20:17; Romans 8:29; Colossians 1:15

with joy as they recognize you in the way you break the bread at the meal and bless God over it, as you must have done many times before in the Sabbath evening ceremony of your people.[2]

Later you come to your disciples in the Upper Room, cowering behind bolted doors. But in your transformed life bolted doors cannot keep you out, nor do time and space limit and control your movement and presence. What laughter and joy there must have been as you uttered the familiar word *Shalom*, a greeting not only of peace but of health, happiness and blessing as well. The mission to the world can now begin, for the divine love has been manifested in the cross and the divine power in the miracle of invincible life. 'As the Father has sent me, so I send you,' you tell them at this first reunion. You must have noticed, dear Lord, their misgiving about their ability to carry out this mission to the world, when they had never been outside their own country. So you breathed on them, inspiring your own love and power, and said they were to preach a Gospel of forgiveness. Breathe your Spirit into me, O Master, to enable me to take my small part in your mission of saving love, wherever I may be.[3]

Dear Lord, I am with Peter when you ask him that three-fold question, so gently but pointedly recalling the three-fold denial. 'Do you really love me?' you ask him and me, and I can only reply with him, 'Lord, you know that I love you!' then hear you say, 'If you really love me, feed my sheep and tend my lambs!' Good Shepherd of souls, we are all your sheep, sometimes lost through our own foolishness, sometimes lost through ignorance and happenings over which we have no control, sometimes lost through sin and self-will. Give me a shepherd's heart, dear Lord, the grateful heart of one who has been found by you, and wants to gather others in to share the love of the Father, and to rejoice in

2. Luke 24:13–35
3. Luke 20:19–23

the other folds where the sheep also belong to you.[4]

O Christ, my Lord, often like Thomas I want proof of your resurrection, I want to see with my physical eyes the wounds of the cross on your glorified body. Open the eyes of faith in me, that I may see you present, open my spiritual ears that I may hear you speaking within. Let me find you in the depths of my being, through your indwelling Spirit. Let me talk with you, listen to you, enjoy you, and so here and now prepare for the life that is eternal, when I finally pass over the horizon of sight and am led to the presence of the Father, your much-loved Father and mine and the Father of all.[5]

4. John 21:15–17; Luke 15
5. John 20:24–29

46. More Experiences

1 Corinthians 15:8. *In the end he appeared even to me.* (N.E.B.)

O Christ, my Lord, the personal experience of your resurrection did not cease with the first few weeks, nor was it limited to your twelve apostles, though the qualification for a successor to poor Judas was judged to be one who had been with you throughout your ministry and one who could witness to your resurrection.[1]

There was Stephen, who first perceived the radical difference that you were to make in the religious ideas and customs of religious people, and so aroused the hostility of many who were unwilling to change. Dear Lord, I see in him the power of your cross as he prayed for those who were stoning him, and I see the power of your resurrection as he saw the heavens opened and you standing in the place of power with God, standing to strengthen your faithful, heroic servant.[2]

O Risen Master, I rejoice that Paul on the Damascus road claimed that his vision of you was of the same order as the experience of the first apostles, and that this was to be his qualification for apostleship.

I rejoice, dear Lord, that this was not his only experience of you as the Everliving One, for at Corinth facing great opposition he experienced your presence, bidding him not to be afraid, for you had many believers in that great city. Again, in the storm and shipwreck on his way to Rome as a prisoner, he had seen you and heard you assuring him of the safety of all in the ship and of your protection for himself

1. Acts 1:22
2. Acts 6:13–14, 7:54–60

so that he could stand before Caesar and be your witness.[3]

He wants, dear Lord, to assure himself of the reality of these experiences, so he lists the earlier witnesses – Peter, all the original twelve, then his brother James of whom as I read the new Scriptures I get the idea that he was very matter-of-fact, down-to-earth, perhaps even sceptical. The experience was not confined to the inner few, for he quotes an appearance to over 500 brethren at once. Dear Lord, I am always moved by his reference to himself, 'Last of all he appeared to me also,' and I take that to apply to every disciple and so to myself, for it is not enough to rely only on the word of others.[4]

Peter blesses your God and Father for your resurrection and speaks of all of us being re-born to a living hope through it, and more movingly says of you, 'whom not having seen we love'. I often wonder, dear Lord, why you did not appear to opponents, critics and sceptics, and after years of puzzling I come to see that it is in the spiritual dimension that our eyes can see, and that love enables us to recognize you. I have come to realize that thought alone cannot reach you, love too is necessary, to pierce clouds of unknowing.[5]

I think also of the writer of the letter to the early Hebrew Christians, who recalls the great army of martyrs before your coming into our human life, who died in bare faith without the knowledge of your resurrection. I am greatly comforted by his words about Moses, 'he endured as seeing him who is invisible', and by his confidence that we are surrounded by this great cloud of witnesses, eager that we should allow nothing to impede us, as we keep our eyes on you the author of our faith and its perfecter.[6]

O Christ, my Lord, I recognize people in my own genera-

3. Acts 9:1–9, 18:9–10, 27:23
4. 1 Corinthians 15:1–9
5. 1 Peter 1:3–5, 8
6. Hebrews 11:27, 12:1–2

tion who, with sure faith in you and confident of eternal life beyond death, have been ready to meet death unafraid, people of every race and nation – some simple souls whom I have known, other more famous souls, some who would not call themselves Christians, but have been faithful and heroic, who will be thanked and welcomed by you. And, dear Lord, I remember the many thousands who went to the gas chambers, broken in body but not in spirit. I sometimes get the sound of the trumpets on the other side, another side only to us, not to you, for you are for ever on both sides of the river.[7]

Dear Risen Master, I thank you for this assurance from you and your heroic witnesses, and I thank you for the experience of your presence and your grace.

7. Hebrews 11:32–40

47. Resurrection Now

Ephesians 3:17, 19. *That Christ may dwell in your
hearts by faith . . . that ye might be filled with all
the fullness of God.*   (A.V.)

O Christ, my Lord, some of your disciples think that
resurrection only takes place after death and that eternal
life is reserved for the next world. I learn from you that both
can be experienced and enjoyed now, a foretaste of the
good things prepared by God for those who love him,
which eye has not seen, nor ear heard, nor the human heart
imagined.[1]

Your disciple Paul talks of being risen with you which pre-
supposes that we have already died with you. Resurrection
makes possible a new birth, a new heart, a new set of values,
a new centre, a new goal, all things which you said are
necessary for membership in the Kingdom of God. To be
with you in your resurrection milieu means that I am a new
creature living in a new dimension, and that all things have
become new. You are now living in the depth of my being
to enlighten, inspire, guide and strengthen me.[2]

I am no longer the prisoner of my environment, subject to
external conditioning, no longer at the mercy of circumstances, external pressures, inner fears and selfishnesses. In
all that happens I can be victorious through your strengthening and nothing can separate me from your love.[3]

I am liberated by you, dear Lord, into a freedom of the
spirit, where I am freed from all lesser loyalties to love your
God and mine with all my heart, mind, soul and strength,

1. 1 Corinthians 2:9
2. Colossians 3:1–4; 2 Corinthians 5:16–17
3. Romans 8:31–39

and to love others not only as I love myself, in equal justice, but with something of your unfailing love.[4]

Risen with you, dear Lord, I begin to share something of your mind, your world view, your attitude to others and to all that happens. Your mind was so unbrokenly centred on God, in complete harmony with him and with your environment. You were completely free from self-preoccupation. You were never hurried, never worried, never muddled, never on the edge of a breakdown as so many of us are, for your mind was anchored in God. You were at ease with everyone you met. Give me, dear Master, that approachable spirit.[5]

You told your first disciples that you had shared with them all that you had heard from the Father, so that they were friends rather than servants. You said that they were to remain united to you as the branches to the vine, so that your strength could flow into them and enable them to bear fruit for you. I learn year after year, dear Lord, that the things I plan and choose in my own wisdom and self-confidence seldom bear spiritual fruit, but that trusting you there is nothing that I cannot venture to do.[6]

Let me see, dear glorified Lord, with your beloved disciple in exile, the door standing open in heaven so that I can see the worship of angels and saints, see you at work in all that happens to redeem every situation and bring good out of every seeming evil, let me see how the kingdoms of the world are slowly but surely becoming the Kingdom which is God's and yours. Let me hear you saying, 'It is I who am making all things new.'[7]

O Christ, my Lord, let me be risen with you in present resurrection, let me share your victorious life and have your mind, let me grow towards a full-grown being, a

4. James 1:25, 2:12; John 8:36; 2 Corinthians 3:17
5. 1 Corinthians 2:16
6. John 15:14–15; Philippians 4:13
7. Revelation 4:1, 7:9–12, 11:15, 21:5

spiritually mature disciple, rooted and grounded in your love, sharing something of your fullness, and being prepared for the place which you are preparing for us.[8]

8. Ephesians 4:13–16

PART VIII
Faith

48. Three Portraits

John 20:31. *These are written that you may believe
that Jesus is the Christ, the Son of God, and that
believing you may have life in his name.* (R.S.V.)

O Christ, my Lord, nowhere do we find a description of what
you looked like. You must have been strong to work as a
carpenter-builder, and to lead the life of a wandering
teacher without a settled home. You must have drawn
people to you, people from all walks of life, particularly
those first twelve disciples, who in spite of misunderstand-
ings, worldly hopes and fears, remained faithful, knowing
that there was no one else who could give meaning to life
and speak with such self-authenticating authority about
God, his Kingdom and his wise, loving will. They learned
from you the kind of people they could become and the
kind of world that the Creator Father wanted to be built.

Dear Lord, we do not have a photograph of you and you
left nothing written, but we do have three portraits and one
deeply moving interpretation of your significance in the
eternal purpose of God and in the inner life of all who come
in touch with you. These portraits are gospels to us, for they
convey such good news from God, expressed so imaginatively that even the simplest person can understand. In
fact you tell us that without simplicity of heart we shall
never understand, and that to enter the Kingdom we have
to become as children, simple-hearted, wondering and trust-
ful, and that if in the course of life we have allowed that
native childlikeness to be overlaid with pride and self-
sufficiency, we need continually to be reborn.

Lord, I like the directness of Mark, giving a short, easily
remembered outline of your ministry and Passion, said by
some earlier disciples to be a summary of the preaching of

135

his uncle Peter. If your last meal took place in the Upper Room of his mother's home, he may have been sent to the garden to warn you of betrayal and danger of arrest. I am grateful for the memory of words which you actually used – *Abba*, Father – *Talitha kumi*, little one arise – *Eloi, Eloi, lama sabachthani*, My God! My God! why hast thou forsaken me – and the explanation of Jewish customs. I am comforted, too, that Mark had a sad failure from which he recovered, so that he became valuable to his sternest critic.

Dear Lord, I find in the gospel of Matthew much of your teaching, supplementing the factual outline of Mark, and I note how it aims to show how truly you fulfil the highest hopes and aspirations of the Law and the Prophets. Lord, I am grateful for his collection of your teaching in the Sermon on the Mount showing the Law written in the heart, but I grieve at my own failure and that of many other disciples to embody its spirit in personal life and in community relations.

I rejoice, dear Master, that the third portrait was painted in words by a Gentile, thought to be both a doctor and an artist. Luke had never met you, but he was eager to find out about you from those who had met you in the flesh. He showed your relevance to the whole world and was eager to make clear your compassion and love for the poor, the despised, the outcast and the heretic, and in his second book he saw how you continued to carry on the work depicted in the gospels through your risen life and spiritual presence, until at length the good news reached Rome and the Emperor.

O Christ, my Lord, I recognize that these basic documents are not biographies as we today write and read them, I realize that it is difficult to be completely sure that any particular saying has come down to us in the authentic words in which you originally spoke it, or with the meaning you originally intended. But from them I get light for the mind, guidance for action, assurance of unfailing love, and as I gaze on the varying portraits and relate to them your presence within my own spirit, I am quickly and gratefully confident that I have come to know you and through you the Father, a happening which you yourself described as eternal life, the highest kind of life, most satisfying and indestructible. Dear Lord, as Peter said, you do indeed have the secret of eternal life, the highest kind of life, because it is the life of the Eternal Father.

49. Intimate Disciple

1 John 1:1. Something which has existed since the beginning, that we have heard, and we have seen with our own eyes; that we have watched and touched with our hands: the Word, who is life – this is our subject. (J.B.)

O Christ, my Lord, he spoke of himself as the disciple whom you loved, and from his writings we see that he was reciprocally the disciple who loved you. He loved you because you first loved him, and he learned from you the nature of love.[1]

He had been one of the inner three who had been with you when you restored the little daughter of the president of the synagogue to life, when you were transfigured and the divine glory shone through, and when you underwent that agony of spirit in the garden of Gethsemane. He was the only one of the twelve to stand by the cross, and it was to him that you committed the care of your mother.[2]

He perceived that you had come from the heart of the Father, that you were the Eternal Word spoken by the Father to reveal his nature and love, for ever verifying the conviction expressed in the words heard at the transfiguration, 'This is my beloved Son, listen to Him.'[3]

His short years with you in the flesh were an unforgettable experience, and loving communion with you over a long life made him see your eternal significance. He always saw the inner meaning of the signs that you did, as in the feeding

1. John 13:23, 19:26, 20:2, 21:20; 1 John 4:16–21
2. Mark 5:37, 9:2, 14:33; John 19:25–27
3. John 1:18; Mark 9:7

of the hungry crowd; he came to faith in you as the Bread of Life which nourishes the inner life of your followers and is available for all. O Master, I pray with John and those first disciples, 'Lord, give us this bread always.'[4]

He treasured your description of yourself as the Good Shepherd, whose sheep recognize your voice and whom you protect with your own life. He knew you to be the door through which your sheep go in and out in safety. Dear Lord, let me go through you as the door to the Father.[5]

By the tomb of Lazarus he heard you say that you were both the resurrection and the life which he saw confirmed in the restoration of Lazarus to life. O Master, let me believe this saying as I come close to death, or as I minister as your representative at the funerals of your disciples.[6]

I am grateful, dear Lord, to this beloved and loving disciple for preserving your reply to Philip, as he groped to understand your revealing of the Father as the Way, the Truth and the Life. Lord, let me not stray from you who are the way, nor ever distrust you who are the truth, nor rest in any other thing than you, who are the life.[7]

Dear Master, this beloved disciple saw in you the Light of the World, and in your healing of a blind man the opening of the eyes of the spirit to see the meaning of yourself. O Lord, I picture the wonder in the face of the blind man at his first sight of a human face, your face. When you ask a blind man, 'What do you want me to do for you,' I reply eagerly with him, 'Master, let me receive my sight.'[8]

Master, let me watch with John through the hours of the cross, see your pain of body and spirit, hear your words of forgiveness, desolation, trust and love, see how you glorified

---

4. 1 John 1:1–4; John 6:34–35
5. John 10:11–16
6. John 11:25–27
7. John 14:5–9
8. John 9; Mark 10:51

the Father, and witness how the Father glorified you. O my dear Lord, I see there love to the uttermost, love for the whole world, for the souls of every generation, and for me, your unworthy but loving disciple.

50. Late Disciple

Acts 27:23. *Whose I am, and whom I serve.* (A.V.)

O Christ, my Lord, Paul had never met you in the flesh, so his experience was much the same as mine. He had seen and heard Stephen's consciousness of your presence and his prayer for his murderers, so like your first word from the cross.

With all his learning he had a simple trusting love and spoke of his relationship to you as 'whose I am and whom I serve'. In his letters he speaks of himself as your servant, called by you, loved by you and sent out as your apostle.[1]

In all his adventures and sufferings he realizes that he has been able to bear everything for you and in you, and he glories in his weakness, recognizing that it is only when he is weak that he is in the happy condition of having to rely on you. He also knows that nothing can separate him from your love, and that your love is identical with the love of God. It is from you, dear Lord, that he has learned the meaning and eternal value of love, and I never cease to wonder that one with such greatness, such ability, such courage, such power of argument, such readiness to rebuke, should have written that amazing hymn of love.[2]

O my Lord, you became the chief value in his life, everything else seemed just worthless compared with his devotion to you. Prison did not daunt his spirit, but he saw in the enforced leisure the opportunity to write some of those priceless letters which showed his understanding of you and

1. 1 Corinthians 15:8–9; Acts 22:10, 27:23
2. 2 Corinthians 11:22–30; Romans 8:31–39; 1 Corinthians 13

your significance for the whole world and the whole of history. Death was nothing less than being with you, preferable even to life. As the time drew near he could look back, conscious of loyal faith and faithful effort, and confident about the joy ahead. He had come to know you in experience.[3]

He painfully learned that he could not attain to holiness and love in his own strength or be saved by inflexible rules. The true life was to be one under the Spirit. He knew that the greatest gifts of the spirit were those characteristics seen in you, and among these love was the greatest and most permanent.[4]

He had had to struggle to believe that one who had died in weakness and shame could possibly be the Christ of God, and it was only after months of inner conflict that he had come to surrender to you as Lord. Then in the bursting light within, he had seen that the essence of conversion and discipleship lay in the question, 'What shall I do, Lord?'

He was the first, dear Lord, to realize your significance for Gentiles as well as for Jews, and from the earliest days of his new life felt your call go out to the world, to enlarge the earliest people of God and to open your Kingdom and salvation to all.[5]

Dear Lord, without you he might have been still a great man, a scholar and theologian, but he would have been a hard man, self-confident, perhaps arrogant. With you he became humble, penitent and loving, quietly confident that in your strength he could face any danger, endure every hardship, become all things to all men, knowing that he would do everything in your company.

Lord, let me confidently ask with him what you want me to do with my life or what is left of it, let me rely on your

3. Philippians 3:7–10, 1:23; 2 Timothy 1:12, 4:6–8
4. Galatians 5:22–23
5. Acts 22:17, 18, 21

strength in the adventures ahead, let me be loving and humble, let me share your vision and his for the world today, and give myself to work for its advancement and completion.

51. The Christ

Luke 24:26. *Was the Messiah not bound to suffer thus before entering upon his glory?* (N.E.B.)

O Christ, my Lord, you began your ministry at a time when there was considerable speculation and expectation about the Messiah. Many wondered if John the Baptist was this expected one, and his firm refusal of the title must have made many look to you, especially when he spoke of his unworthiness, his conviction that you would baptize with the Spirit as well as with water, and that his influence would decrease as your authority grew. You spoke of him as the greatest born of human parentage, but implied that we could enjoy a spiritual birth much more significant.[1]

Dear Lord, you were grateful to Peter for his impression of you as the long-expected Messiah, but very severe when he wanted to impose on you his own ideas of messiahship. You forbade those first believers to speak openly of you as the Christ at that early stage. Was it because you knew of the popular expectations of a worldly ruler, of achieving Israel's liberation by force and revolution? – an interpretation which you rejected in your forty days' exploration of the Father's will.[2]

You made it clear that your Kingdom was one of truth and love, operating in the hearts and minds of people first of all, and then leavening all their relationships and activities. The qualifications for membership were penitence in a deep change of heart, and faith in God, his completely righteous and loving will, and your mission from him to establish his Kingdom of the Spirit. Dear Lord, I want to

1. John 1:19–23; Mark 1:7–8; John 3:29–30; Matthew 11:9–11
2. Matthew 16:13–20; Mark 9:9–13

144

qualify, help me to do so within my own spirit where you operate.[3]

Lord, I have the intuition that your deep study of your Bible gave you the perception that the Messiah was to be a Suffering Servant who would win the world by loving service, suffering and death, win spiritual victory. I see that your conception of Christhood demanded the vindication of voluntarily accepted death, if that should come and if you believed it to be the Father's method of redemption. I dare to wonder if you only became the Christ at the moment of death, which could also be the moment of resurrection, ascension to God and liberation to be a universal presence of love and saving grace.[4]

I seem to see, dear Lord, in the coming of those Greeks during the last week, a temptation to evade the cross, perhaps by a mission to the wider world, and my heart leaps at your resolution that just as there can be no crop in nature without the death of the seed, so there can be no harvesting of souls without the death of God's Son and representative.[5]

A few days later, my Lord, with the suffering and death of the cross undergone with unfailing love, in your first reunion with the disciples you sent them out to the world with the words, 'As the Father has sent me, so I send you.' Now you are not only the glory of Israel but the Christ of the world. Now you have the authority of fulfilled messiahship – O Christ, my Lord and Master, you call and we respond, you command and we obey, you lead and we follow – to the Father, then to the world, both with you.[6]

3. John 3:3–5
4. Isaiah 52:13 – 53:12
5. John 12:20–32
6. John 20:19–23

52. Son of God

*Luke 2:49. Did you not know that I must be busy
with my Father's affairs?* (J.B.)

O Christ, my Lord, was it on your visit to Jerusalem for the
Passover, as a boy of twelve years old, that you first became
conscious of your intimate relationship with God? Perhaps
it was at that Passover that you became a Son of the Law,
with childlike spirit and clear-eyed faith, so obvious to the
rabbis with whom you talked, which suggested a deeper
relationship, Son to the divine giver of the Law as well. In
the light of what happened on that visit you gently re-
proached your parents for not looking for you in the
Father's house when they feared you lost. Perhaps it was
then that you realized the purpose of life, as doing the
Father's will, carrying out the Father's work.[1]

It was in those hidden years at Nazareth that you began
to greet God as *Abba*, the affectionate familiar way in which
any Jewish boy, now as then, addresses his father. I can hear
you calling out *Abba* to Joseph when you wanted to attract
his attention or say something to him. Your disciples are
grateful to Joseph that his fatherly care of you should lead
on so naturally to the thought of God as Father. Your
interpreter Paul says that it is through your Spirit that we
are enabled to say '*Abba*, Father', because we have been
adopted as God's dear children. So with you, dear Lord, I
cry out in love '*Abba*, Father', Father, dear Father, your
Father and mine.[2]

In your baptism in the Jordan near Jericho your Sonhood
was confirmed by the inner voice, 'Thou art my beloved

1. Luke 2:41–54
2. Mark 14:36; Romans 8:15; Galatians 4:6

Son, in whom I am well pleased,' and by the descent of the Spirit, attesting the anointing as the Christ of God. In the forty days following, you resisted doubts about this experience as well as temptations to use the Spirit's power in ways that would have defeated the will of the Father. The same voice came again in the night of glory on Mount Tabor, when you faced the likelihood of suffering and death.[3]

Somehow the sick in spirit and deranged in mind perceived your spiritual authority, and cried out in alarm at your challenge to release those imprisoned in the grip of evil.[4]

Dear Lord, I tremble at the opposition of the rigidly 'orthodox', who condemned your assurance as God's Son as blasphemy, worthy of death. At that stage they could not know of your obedience unto death, proving you were truly God's Son by the things you suffered. Nor would they agree later with the faith of one of their number that the final vindication came in the resurrection, which declared both your Sonship and Christhood.[5]

The word 'Father' was constantly on your lips, dear Lord, and exemplified in your ministry, for you said that you always spoke the words which you heard the Father speaking, and did the deeds which you saw the Father always willing and performing. At the tomb of your friend Lazarus, you thanked the Father that he heard your prayer on that occasion and added your grateful confidence that he always heard you. You were always one with the Father in heart and mind and will.[6]

God was always the great priority in your thinking. You believed that you came from him and would return to him, and always be with him. You acknowledged the priority

3. Mark 1:10–11, 9:7
4. Mark 3:11–12
5. Hebrews 5:7–10; Romans 1:1–4
6. John 11:41–42

of the Father, you prayed to the Father as your God, you acknowledged that the Father was greater than yourself. It was God whose power raised you from the dead and exalted you to glory at God's right hand, in both authority and never ceasing activity: 'My Father is working even until now and I work.' The fact that you would be with the Father and that your disciples would see you no more with their physical eyes, should make their hearts rejoice, for even greater things would happen than those they had already seen. So we fix our eyes and hopes on the spiritual and eternal, where you are with the Father in the sphere of perfect love, holiness and power.[7]

Dear Lord, you associate us with yourself as children of God, our Father as well as your Father. You are the firstborn among many brethren, the firstborn of all creation, the firstborn from the dead. O Christ, my Lord, I can never be thankful enough for you.[8]

7. John 5:19–20; Colossians 3:1
8. Romans 8:29; Colossians 1:15, 18

53. The Servant

Isaiah 42:1. Behold my servant, whom I uphold, my chosen, in whom my soul delights. (R.S.V.)

O Christ, my Lord, you must often have studied the servant passages in Isaiah, often and deeply, and found in them the inspiration of your ministry and the assurance that if in obedience to that call suffering and death should come, it would not be the final word. The God whose servant you were would justify you and make your death redemptive, as he did in the case of that earlier servant.[1]

I can see, O my Lord, how you accepted as the conditions of spiritual victory readiness to identify yourself with sinful men as you did in your baptism, willingness to accept suffering and sacrifice as the divine way, bearing the sin of individuals and humanity on your heart and always interceding for them as you did upon the cross.[2]

O Christ, my Lord, I know how difficult it is for even your most devoted servants to accept suffering as the Father's way of saving the world. It is easy, dear Lord, to accept it in theory when all is going well and our efforts seem to be making some impression, but it is much more difficult when misunderstanding, misinterpretation, mistakes and failures seem to be the consequence of our efforts in discipleship.

Lord, your own people interpret those great passages in Isaiah as fulfilled in their own history of suffering and persecution. They don't accept our claim that they were fulfilled in you, perhaps because they don't see them being

1. Isaiah 42:1–4, 49:1–6, 50:4–9, 52:13–53:12; Matthew 8:17; Acts 4:27–31
2. Isaiah 53:12

fulfilled in us. O Lord, help your Church to be a servant community, not only to individuals who identify themselves with it but to all other communities, to other faiths, to secular societies who try to minister to the needs and sufferings of humanity.

Dear Lord, help your Church to bear the sins of the world as you did, to have your compassion with suffering people, to be ready to give its life for the world and its great resources to bring healing and relief. Help us to see that the world will only be won by loving sacrifice and suffering, that the cross must be at the centre of our life in every generation, as it has been in the heart of the Father since the beginning of creation.

And help me, dear Lord, to be a servant to our God and Father, answering his call, relying on his grace, trusting that my little unworthy service may advance his Kingdom in some small way, bringing a little comfort, healing and love to those who see in pain nothing but pain. Help them and me to glimpse the brightness of Easter from the darkness of our Good Fridays.

54. Divine Model

Hebrews 1:3. *He is the radiant light of God's glory and the perfect copy of his nature.* (J.B.)

O Christ, my Lord, your disciples today often say with Philip, 'Show us the Father and we shall be content.' Your reply to us is the same as it was to him, 'He who has seen me has seen the Father.' You are the divine model, not only of the Father's being and nature, but of his will and activity. You have told us that you speak what you hear the Father saying, and do what you see the Father always doing. You have told us that the Father is always at work, that you too are always active in the same way. We must not think that our activity on his behalf is the only force at work – he and you are working, often unseen and behind the scenes, to further his eternal purpose of love, both for each much loved soul and for the whole world.[1]

Like Moses, dear Lord, we long to see God. I cannot believe with earlier thinkers that man cannot see God and live, for you yourself have promised the blessing that the single-hearted, the whole-hearted shall see God, and your saints have longed for the beatific vision. In the past devout seekers have thought of God under various symbols. That of fire has attracted many, for fire gives light and warmth and energy, it refines, it attracts attention, it kindles and spreads; a brightly burning flame speaks of activity. With Moses I stand at the burning bush, and marvel at its paradox of burning without being consumed, and I remember your longing that the divine fire would kindle and spread: 'I came to cast fire upon the earth; and would that

1. John 14:9

151

it were already kindled!'[2]

You yourself, dear Lord, spoke of the wind as a symbol of the Kingdom, blowing when and where it will, and you breathed your spiritual breath on your disciples on that great Easter reunion, reminding them of the Father's breath of life when he brought man into being. When they experienced your indwelling Spirit they thought of it as brightly burning flames lighting on each, and as the wind blowing in strength.[3]

Helpful as these symbols are, they are not as satisfying as the insight of John and Paul and the unnamed writer of Hebrews, who spoke of you as the image of God. 'No man has ever seen God,' says John, 'the only Son who is in the heart of the Father, he has made him known.' You are the image of the invisible God, says Paul, while the writer whose aim is to interpret you to his Jewish brethren says that you reflect the glory of God and bear the very stamp of his nature. O Christ, my Lord, if the Eternal Father is like you, my heart is at peace.[4]

Your beloved disciple gives us another insight when he speaks of you as the Eternal Word become human, so that we judge all other words which claim to be the word of the Lord by you, and we see how you fulfil all that is true, and correct and complete all that is not fully so.[5]

So, dear Lord, we have a representation of the Father in terms of a human life – not only in his nature and character, but in his will and activity. I love to think of you as the divine representative, bringing good news from the Eternal Father, speaking his will, acting on behalf of him, doing those things that he is always doing.

As your disciple, O Lord, I pray that I too may represent the Father in some small way, taking you as the pattern,

2. Matthew 5:8; Luke 12:49
3. John 3:8; Genesis 2:7; John 20:22
4. John 1:18; Colossians 1:15; Hebrews 1:3
5. John 1:14

and having you in the depths of my being, to show me how to do this truly and faithfully, in the world of today with all its changing conditions, its confusions and rebellions, its fears and tensions and hopes. Let me do this with quiet joy, unshakeable faith and unfailing love, O Christ sent from God.

55. The First Paraclete

John 14:16. *I will pray the Father, and he shall give you another Comforter, that he may abide with you for ever.* (A.V.)

O Christ, my Lord, I realize that in your coming something new happened, which did not just operate for a short time only to be withdrawn, but something continuous and permanent, an unveiling of what is always going on in the spiritual and the eternal.

When you were with your first disciples, they knew that they could come to you in any emergency or need, whether in concern for those in trouble or on occasions when guidance was needed.

They knew that when burdened and hard-pressed they could find renewing strength in you, a faith made more explicit in your later apostle Paul, who, in an adventurous life of hardship and danger, knew that nothing could separate him and all who trust in you from the love of God which was so clearly embodied in you.

Dear Lord, I know that you show me the Father and the Holy Spirit. My mind cannot grasp the mystery of the Godhead, beyond all names, all thought, all words, the Original and Final Reality in whom we live and move and have our being. Through you I experience the Eternal Mystery as Creator and Father, as Saviour and Lord, as Strengthener and Sanctifier, as eternally transcendent, incarnate in time, indwelling our inmost being, always above me and with me and in me.

I find it difficult to believe that I can do greater things than you, though I can accept that with the omnipresent Spirit, you have an army of loving disciples and that in our uniting there will be a greater power than just the addition of our individual obedience, as shown in your assurance that when even two or three are gathered together in your spirit and as your disciples there you too will be present and active.

You promised that the Second Paraclete would show us things to come. Dear Master, I pray that I am not mistaken in believing that the Comforter will show us the meaning of the things that will happen and open to us the Father's purpose and way of working as you did in the resurrection evening when you interpreted to the first disciples the things concerning yourself, with the assurance that everything had been taken up into the Father's purpose, even betrayal and crucifixion. Also, dear Lord, like some of the earlier prophets, I believe that when I look at attitudes and actions through your eyes I can see a consequence of blessing or loss.

Let the new Paraclete put into our minds intuition of truth, good desires and actions of love, as you did when you were physically present, and may he strengthen us to bring them to good effect, as you encouraged our elder brethren in discipleship to do.

John 14:16–18, 15:1–8, 14:7, 1:50, 14:12–14

56. Gatherer

John 11:52. *To gather together the scattered children of God.* (N.E.B.)

O Christ, my Lord, I see in your instruction to your first disciples after the feeding of the hungry crowd east of Jordan, to 'gather up the fragments that nothing be lost', a characteristic of your mind and of the eternal activity of the Father. I see included in your care the little scraps of humanity that die before they have had a chance to live, the outcasts from society, the myriad casualties of history, the many souls who seem lost with no one to care for them.

I thrill at the thought that you will gather into one not only your own people but the children of God scattered throughout the world. As the shepherd of souls you speak of gathering sheep from other folds, that we may all come into the one flock of the Father Shepherd.

I rejoice, dear Lord, in the insight of your apostle and servant Paul, that God's secret and eternal purpose has been revealed in you, to sum up all things through you, both earthly and heavenly, all truths and all people, gathering the whole of humanity into the unity of the divine love.

O Master, on the night before you died, you prayed for your disciples that they might all be one, with the unity that the Father shared with you. And you prayed into the future that all who believed through those past disciples should be united in love in the same perfection of unity.

O Christ, you must weep over your Church today, with its divisions and rivalries, its preoccupation with its own separated life, as you wept over Jerusalem and the failure of its Temple to be a centre of prayer for all nations. O Lord of the Church, I pray for the unity of your will and that our eyes may be opened to see your way to that unity. O Master, help the Church to be a community of love within itself and in its relation to other communities of faith. May it be a servant community, with eyes open to the Father's activity everywhere, and rejoicing in the experience and treasures of others. May all take their part in sharing and receiving the treasures the Eternal Father has given! May we all be drawn into your own ecumenical movement and into the service of humanity!

O Crucified Master, people everywhere are drawn to the love seen in the cross, a love that knows no boundaries and still remains invincible love, whatever we do to you. O Saving Master, humanity needs a universal high priest, who carries the world in his heart, who stands before God on behalf of all, and before the world on behalf of God.

O Shepherd of Souls, your disciples see in you one who unites us in life and gathers us in death, conducting us into a beyond closer to the Creator and Saviour of all, enfolding us all in the divine embrace and infusing into us something of the eternal love.

John 6:12 – gathering up the fragments
John 10:6 – gathering other sheep
John 11:49–52 – gathering all the children of God
John 12:32–33 – the magnet of the cross
Ephesians 1:10, 3:4–5 – God's long-term plan to gather everything into Christ
Revelation 7:9–10 – gathered in from every race and nation

57. The New Adam

1 Corinthians 15:45. *The first man Adam became a living being; the last Adam became a life-giving spirit.* (R.S.V.)

O Christ, my Lord, your favourite way of referring to yourself was 'Son of man'. Sometimes it seems to mean just 'man', emphasizing your full humanity. You were sometimes tired, hungry or thirsty, you slept on the boat crossing the Sea of Galilee, you wept at the grave of your friend. You were grateful for the loyalty of your disciples, you asked for their support in Gethsemane, you felt desolate and forsaken on the cross, you underwent all the temptations that ordinary men have to face, yet without succumbing to them. You died. You were made like us your brethren in every respect.[1]

At other times, dear Lord, this name for yourself seemed to have a deeper meaning, with a note of divine authority, as when Daniel saw in the night visions one who came to the Ancient of Days, the Eternal, and dominion and glory was given to him, and a kingdom that should never pass away or be destroyed. It was of this you spoke before the high priest when you claimed that he would see you seated at the right hand of power and coming on the clouds of heaven. Your martyr Stephen was equally explicit, for he identifies the Son of man standing with God as you.[2]

Your servant Paul speaks of you as the new Adam, the first of a new race of men. The first Adam was a man of dust, the second Adam is from heaven; the first Adam was a living being, the new Adam a life-giving Spirit. In our

1. Luke 22:38-40; Hebrews 2:17, 4:15
2. Daniel 7:13-15; Matthew 26:64; Acts 7:55-56, 59-60

human solidarity in Adam we all die, in our incorporation
into you we are all made alive. I think again of Paul's
further insight that when we are incorporated spiritually
into you, we become new creatures, enabled to live in a new
creation.[3]

You, dear Lord, show us completed man, man as God
always meant him to be, man as he can become by your
grace. Above all, we are meant to be embodiments of love,
imitations of you. 'We know', O Lord, with the apostle of
love, 'that whoever loves is born of God and knows God'
and that 'he who abides in love abides in God, and God
abides in him'. We know, too, dear Lord, that when we love
we have passed out of the sphere of death into the sphere of
life.[4]

Dear Lord, you have made us all the people of God,
brought us into the Father's family, made us citizens of the
commonwealth of heaven in which all distinctions of race,
culture, class, economic status or social superiority are done
away. We are a new race in you, sharing a new nature. You
restore the divine image which is the Creator Father's will,
and which has become defaced by weakness, sin and self-
will. You admit us into a spiritual democracy in which the
Spirit is made available for all – not only for prophets,
priests and rulers, but for young and old alike, men, women
and children, employers and employed.[5]

The gates of the City of God are never shut and the
crowd around the throne where you are enthroned with the
Father is so great that it cannot be numbered, and is drawn
from all races and nations and languages, an ever-growing
communion of saints. O Master, with you I long that none
may exclude themselves from this great gathering, but that
all may be led by you to the Father's presence and be for
ever embraced in the divine love.[6]

3. 1 Corinthians 15:21–22, 45–47
4. 1 John 4:7, 16, 3:14
5. Colossians 3:10–12
6. Revelation 21:24–26, 7:9–10

58. Judge?

John 3:17. *For God sent not his Son into the world to condemn the world; but that the world through him might be saved.* (A.V.)

O Christ, my Lord, all down the generations since your first coming your disciples have believed that you would come again at the end of time in undeniable glory, to judge both the living and the dead. Peter speaking to Cornelius says that he and the other witnesses were commanded by you to testify that you were ordained by God to be the judge of all, and Paul writing to the Christians in Rome speaks of the day when God shall judge the secrets of men by you, and warns that we shall all stand before your judgement seat.[1]

Yet you, dear Lord, were emphatic that the primary purpose of your coming was not judgement and certainly not condemnation. In clear and simple words you said, 'I came not to judge the world but to save the world.' Your beloved disciple, who more than any other understood your mind, expressed this conviction in words that have become the very heart of the Gospel – God so loved the world that he gave you, his Son, that through faith in you none should perish, but have eternal life, explicitly adding that the Father's purpose was not to condemn but to save.[2]

In all my grateful confidence for this assurance, O Master, I realize that I am judged when I stand before you, and that in the burning light of your holiness and love, I see how far short I fall of the Father's glory and will. With Peter I cry out, 'Depart from me, for I am a sinful man, O Lord,' but

1. Acts 10:42; Romans 2:6, 14:10
2. John 3:16–17, 12:47

knowing that this is the last thing I want to happen. With that earlier prophet in his vision of the worship of heaven, I cry out, 'Woe is me! For I am lost . . . for my eyes have seen the King, the Lord of hosts!' and with the penitent psalmist I pray, 'Create in me a clean heart, O God, and put a new and right spirit within me.' I begin to realize that to sin against law is grievous, to sin against the light of conscience, imperfect though it be, is more grievous, and to sin against love is most grievous of all.[3]

Standing before you, dear Lord, the expression in human terms of the righteousness, holiness and love of the Father, I come to see that judgement, when it comes, both now or at the moment of death, or at the final consummation, will be largely self-judgement. It will not be a case of a poor confused man in the dock, anxious and uncertain about the verdict, but an incontrovertible judgement pronounced by me myself, with no possible plea of not guilty. There can be only one plea – 'Guilty, my Lord'. At some point, dear holy Lord, the books of memory and character will have to be read by me, not in the technique of detailed accountancy, but in the realization of what I really am and the mess I have made of life, the timidities, the hidden hurts, the disguised self-seeking, the failures to accept repeated forgivenesses and the neglect of opportunities of grace offered by you on behalf of the Father.[4]

Your response, dear Lord, to my plea of guilty, is not to tell me that I am not, but to declare me forgiven, to set me free to make a fresh start, to direct my eyes not to the failures of the past but to the grace of the future. Expecting you to be a stern judge, I hear you addressing me as 'My dear', bidding me go in peace of heart and sin no more, for the Father has put away my sin. So in my self-judgement in the light of your goodness and holiness, the righteousness of God is vindicated, and in the forgiveness wrought through

3. Romans 3:23; Luke 5:8; Isaiah 6:5; Psalm 51:10
4. Revelation 20:12

you the divine love is experienced.[5]

With your servant Paul, I see that the universal and
eternal love became personalized in me and for me through
you. If it happens in me, it can and must be happenable for
every other individual soul. Dear Lord, could I be right in
hoping and thinking that there is no final judgement in the
human sense, that it is never too late? Did you not say that
the Good Shepherd goes on seeking the poor lost sheep until
he finds it, that the woman goes on seeking the coin acci-
dentally lost until she finds it, that the father is always longing and waiting for the wayward son or daughter to return,
ready with the new robe, the ring and the family celebration
of angels and saints and earlier forgiven sinners?[6]

Lord, the disciple most conscious of your love, the see-er
of the eternal, the heavenly, the unchanging, saw a door
standing open in heaven, always open, never to be shut.
Dear Lord, I see another door standing open, never shut –
the door of hell, which on its Godward side is also a door of
heaven, through which all who think themselves prisoners
can at any moment go free. You are both doors, O Christ,
my Lord, and the porter at each, to beckon everyone in and
to welcome us all with the eternal Love.[7]

5. John 8:11
6. Galatians 2:20; Luke 15
7. Revelation 4:1; John 10:7, 9

59. Bread of Heaven

John 6:34. *Lord, give us this bread always.* (R.S.V.)

O Christ, my Lord, I never cease to marvel that on the last night of your physical life, when your heart was heavy with foreboding, your thoughts were with your disciples. You prayed that they might be kept in the Father's truth, guarded from evil, united in love for one another, assured of your indwelling in them as you were conscious of the Father in you. I marvel at your wisdom in attaching to something that they would do regularly the remembrance of your death and later your undying life and love. For on the evening of every Sabbath they would meet as every family of your people did, and bread would be broken and wine taken, and over both God would be blessed for all his goodness. Now, dear Lord, you added the memory of your body broken and your blood shed. You must have taken part in this *Khiddush* a hundred times or more, as father of the family of disciples, and you would be present with them every time they continued this lovely homely ceremony, with the meaning you added to it. They would always recognize you in the breaking of bread and the sharing of the cup.[1]

Dear Lord, there are four accounts of this new command, showing the importance which your first disciples attached to its faithful and loving obedience. Your much-loved disciple does not include an account of the actual adoption of it as the new covenant sealed by your death, but he gives us a full devotional and theological meditation on it, in which he speaks of you as bread of heaven, the true bread for the soul, given by the Father, the spiritual manna which will nourish your people as they journey through life. Dear

1. John 17; 1 Corinthians 11:23–26

Lord, I am grateful again that you gave us a tangible sacramental symbol, in which the thought of our minds and the faith of our souls is confirmed and strengthened by physically receiving bread and wine, to which you add the sharing of your own life, offered on the cross and transformed in the resurrection.[2]

O all-providing Lord, my mind cannot help wondering how this can be so, as did the minds of those who heard you interpret the deeper meaning of the feeding of the hungry crowd. Yet I find as I continue that my mind ceases to wonder and I simply accept that you are the bread of heaven and the wine of life, nourishing, strengthening, invigorating, adding joy and sparkle to daily life. Dear Lord, I now find that I do not feel the urge to pray, as your first disciples did, 'Lord, give us this bread always,' but I thank you for doing so. The experience of your disciples all down the ages is becoming mine also, that every participation is a Eucharist, a thanksgiving for your death and resurrection and exaltation, and for the inner nourishment I receive through it.[3]

Dear Lord, you are the celebrant at every Eucharist, the priest is your representative, it is your authority and transforming power, your pervading love, your shared life. There lies our unity, O Lord, even though we deny it by our separate altar-tables and our differing views on how you mediate your universal ministry. Lord, I pray that you will show us your way to the unity of your will. Lord, I believe in you, help my misgivings about the churches. Grant, dear Lord, that however much and however often we change and revise the setting of worship in which we place your life-sharing action, we may never forget its essential centrality, its life-giving reality.[4]

O Christ, my Lord, I see how, in our obedience to your

2. Mark 14:22–25; Matthew 26:26–29; Luke 22:14–19; John 6:35–40, 47–50
3. John 6:41–42, 52, 34; 1 Kings 19:4–8
4. 1 Corinthians 10:16–17

command, the night of your birth, the night in which you were betrayed, the hours on the cross, the morning when your resurrection was perceived, the glory of your exaltation by God to himself, and our own worship and need are brought together in this timeless moment, a foretaste of the life which is eternal.

PART IX

Interim

60. Collective Body

1 Corinthians 12:27. Now you together are Christ's
body; but each of you is a different part of it.
(J.B.)

O Christ, my Lord, you saw the need of a continuing body
to carry on your caring, loving, saving work, so, following
the precedent of the earlier community of faith, you chose
twelve men to renew and to extend the work of blessing.
The foundation of this extended Church was to be faith in
you as the Messiah and Son of the Living God. Lord, I
accept without doubt or question the claim that you gave
them the keys of the Kingdom of God so that they could
enable people to enter the Kingdom, but I find it difficult to
believe that they were to keep them out, except perhaps to
warn them when they were not yet ready to enter, and thus
to help them to become so.[1]

Dear Lord, could I be right in thinking that you never
envisaged the new community ever displacing the old or
separating from it, though I remember your warnings that
your followers would from time to time be accused of dis-
loyalty, even blasphemy?

In his vision of the eternal Kingdom your disciple of love
saw four-and-twenty elders bowing in the worship of heaven,
both sets of twelve, and in his vision of the holy city, the
new Jerusalem which is the mother of us all, with twelve
foundation stones on which were the names of your twelve
apostles, and twelve gates over which were written the
names of the twelve tribes and which were never shut.[2]

Your disciple Paul thought of the Church as your Body,

1. Matthew 16:13–20
2. Revelation 4:4, 10, 22:12–14

the corporate expression of the personal life which we see in the gospel portraits, meant to be the Christ Community, the Community of Love, the Serving Community. O dear, wise Lord, I pray that it may be so.[3]

You yourself prayed that your disciples should be one, knit together in mutual love; you prayed that they should be sanctified; you made the Church apostolic by sending it out in love to the world to bring in each new generation; you willed that it should be catholic, universal for all and in the fullness of truth. Lord, perhaps we should not concentrate on praying for unity, but instead pray for holiness, in the conviction that if the Church were holy in its members and branches, it would soon become one.[4]

Lord, the Church has not been sufficiently faithful to your example and pattern. It has excommunicated those whom it has labelled heretics, it has burned and tortured those who have differed from its accepted standards of belief. and has deceived itself in thinking that it was doing this for their salvation. It has broken into many fragments, large and small, its branches have claimed that each holds the whole truth, and have followed the example of the original twelve in wanting to be greatest.

Yet, Lord, it has brought something of the love of the Father and the assurance of forgiveness to its members and to the world. It has mediated your grace to unnumbered humble and penitent worshippers, it has cared for the sick and suffering and ministered to the dying, brought comfort to the bereaved, it has tried to feed the hungry, bring release to prisoners, and has stood for the oppressed and the deprived. Further, dear Lord, without the Church I would not have known the Father or you, I would have been lonely and lost, a sheep without a shepherd, and a threat and menace to my fellow humans.

Dear Lord of the Church, your Church is faced in every

3. 1 Corinthians 12:12–31
4. John 17

generation with the choices you saw offered to you in the forty days in the Jordan desert, when you were discovering the Father's will and his way of saving mankind. Being in the world, it has to learn from you that it does not belong to the world and must not be conformed to it. It understandably likes to see its influence acknowledged, it would like to be popular, it is tempted to jump on to any contemporary bandwagon. It finds it easier to be engrossed in planning new structures, absorbed in administration and in the reform of the externals of worship, rather than in deepening its spirituality and holiness or in extending its loving care. Dear Lord, I pray for the Church a prayer that it has preserved for its members to use, a prayer that you will be eager to answer: 'Let thy continual pity cleanse and defend thy Church, and because it cannot continue in safety without thy rescuing grace, preserve it ever more by thy help and goodness.' Amen, dear Lord.[5]

5. John 17:14–16; Romans 12:2; Matthew 23:23; Book of Common Prayer: Trinity 16

61. Worshipping Community

Hebrews 12:22–24. *What you have come to is Mount Zion and the city of the living God, the heavenly Jerusalem where the millions of angels have gathered for the festival, with the whole Church . . . You have come to God himself . . . and been placed with the spirits of the saints who have been made perfect; and to Jesus, the mediator who brings a new covenant.* (J.B.)

O Christ, my Lord, it was your custom to go to the synagogue on the Sabbath day to worship God with your people and to hear the reading of the Law and the Prophets. Your earliest disciples after the withdrawal of your physical presence were continually in the Temple praising God and worshipping you with Him. The growing number of disciples experienced a deep fellowship and were regular in the breaking of bread and in praying together, though later some needed to be urged not to give up regular assembly. Dear Lord, you emphasized the need of true and spiritual worship.[1]

The poets and psalmists of your people constantly spoke of the joy of worship in the Temple, and the prophets warned that worship which did not issue in holy and righteous living was not true worship. David worshipped you in songs on the harp and longed to build you a temple. His son Solomon did so, and prayed for forgiveness for the thought that God could be confined to temples built by men. You, dear Lord, taught us that the divine presence cannot be limited to places of worship, which are sacra-

1. Luke 4:15, 24:52–53; Acts 2:42; Hebrews 10:24–25; John 4:24

mental reminders of the Spirit of the Father which fills the universe. You also assured us that where two or three are gathered as your disciples you will be present with them.[2]

O dear Lord, I learn slowly that the meaning of worship is to give the Father his full worth as Creator and Saviour, to make him the great and central reality of our lives, to love him with all our being, not for his gifts but for what he eternally is, not in the hope of heaven or fear of hell, but for himself alone, to be able to say 'I have no good beyond thee, thou art what I desire above anyone or anything else, thou art the strength of my heart and my portion for ever.'

In worship, dear Master, I submit all my nature to the Father, my conscience is quickened by his holiness, my mind is nourished with his truth, my imagination is purified by his beauty, my heart is open to his love, my will surrendered to his purpose. I realize, dear Lord, that adoration is the most selfless emotion of which my nature is capable, the most effective antidote to my inveterate self-centredness.

I know, dear Lord, that I can worship the Father when I am alone, but that I am helped when I worship in the company of fellow disciples of yours and fellow children of the Father. I know that I can worship anywhere, but that it helps to pray in quiet places, where prayer has been offered for many generations, where the very stones have been witnesses of the sacraments of grace, and the outpourings of simple hearts in penitence, need, love and gratitude.

When your people worship on earth, dear Lord, we are with angels and archangels, with the whole company of heaven, with the spirits of just men made perfect and with an ever-growing communion of saints from every age and every race and every community of faith, and in fellowship with our loved ones who have undergone this final birth

2. 1 Chronicles 16:29; Psalm 29:2, 96:9; Matthew 18:20; Wisdom 1:7

into the spiritual and the eternal.[3]

O Christ, my Lord, I pray that the worship of every congregation of your disciples may be so humble and loving and grateful that if people from outside should over-hear or over-see, they would feel the presence of the Eternal Father and be drawn into the circle of loving fellowship and adoring love. To worship truly, dear Lord, is to be truly saved, and to be prepared for the blessedness which the Father wills for every single child of his and every brother and sister of yours. Let me so live and love and worship now, that after the little sleep of death, I shall see the Father's face, be more conscious of his likeness in the depth of my being and be extremely satisfied with it.[4]

3. Isaiah 6:1–3
4. 1 Corinthians 14:24–25; Psalm 17:15

62. Lord of the Church

Matthew 16:18. *On this rock I will build my Church.*
And the gates of the underworld can never hold out
against it. (J.B.)

O Christ, my Lord, if the Church is indeed your body, we
can be sure that you will always be at work in it and upon
it. We have learned from you that it was out of his great
love for the world that God sent you, and that it was out of
your love for the world that you founded the Church. In a
way, dear Lord, we could say that the world is more dear to
you than the Church. It must live for the world, give its life
for the world, not expecting to be supported by the world,
but assuring people that it will support them in everything
that happens, in every danger that threatens, in every blow
and difficulty, and in every adventure and opportunity.[1]

In every age, dear Lord, there will be new needs to be met
and new tasks to carry out. In our age it seems that a
primary need is human unity, to match the cosmic unity
that is developing so rapidly, in which people move about
the world so much more and so much more quickly, with
news and views flashing round the world in a fraction of a
second, with television showing us what other people are
like and how they live. We are becoming aware of our inter-
dependence, we see how what happens in one country
affects many other countries.

We are learning from bitter experience that modern war-
fare is so destructive, so total and so dehumanizing that we
can no longer accept it as a means of settling disputes
between nations. Prophets have always seen a vision of a
world at peace, where weapons would be turned into

1. John 3:16, 20:20–22; Matthew 28:16–20

agricultural instruments, where tanks would be converted into tractors and combine harvesters, and bombers into transport planes to bring speedy personal help, medicines and food to emergency situations. Dear Lord, you must often weep over our world today.[2]

You are making us realize that chronic problems and injustices untackled and unsolved often lead those who suffer in them to despair and violence. O Christ, Saviour of the world, help us to act while there is still time. Help us to work unceasingly for the unity of humanity, so that we can bear one another's burdens and help to solve one another's problems. We cannot expect this unity to come, dear Lord, unless your Church is united, unless we see that in your design it is to be the pattern for the world's life. You are leading us to unity, we need your Spirit to show us your way to achieve it. We need more prayer for this, rather than expecting you to give us unity which we can perceive and achieve if we are truly your Body. Only then, dear Lord, will the world believe and co-operate in the Father's ecumenical will.[3]

When the Church is united according to your will, it will be able to speak with a united voice. It will be your prophet to the nations, warning them of the consequences of present policies and actions, alerting them to new dangers, and showing its own insights into the Father's will, as well as trying to identify the motives and factors in each human situation so that they may be set right. In this way, dear Lord, it looks as if you intend your Church to be the conscience of the nations, influenced by the Father's righteousness and love.

In one way, O Lord of the Church, you are doing a surprising thing: you have sent it out in world mission, to proclaim the Father's love and to bring good news to people everywhere, the result of which has been the revival of what

2. Micah 4:1–5; Isaiah 2:2–4; Luke 19:41–44
3. Ephesians 1:9–10; John 11:51–52, 17:23

we have thought of as rival faiths. You are making us see that we Christians have no monopoly of you, but that others have their experiences of the Father, only expressed in different ways, in terms of their own ways of thought and through their own cultural expressions. We realize with your disciple Peter that God shows no partiality, but in every nation those who reverence him and do what is right are acceptable to him. Help us, dear Lord, to see the spiritual treasures of the nations joyfully, and with equal joy to share with them our special treasure, the revelation of God in you and the incombustible riches which you bring. Help us to work together with people of other faiths for human welfare, the unity of mankind, social justice for all and peace upon earth.[4]

Dear Lord, the Father Creator has given us a wonderful world, with great beauty, with an endless variety of creatures. Help us to love the earth as you and the Father do, never to exploit or exhaust or pollute it, and to trust that there is further development ahead and even greater joys. Dear Lord, my heart echoes the gloria of your servant Paul: 'O the depth of the riches and wisdom and knowledge of God! How unsearchable are his judgements and how inscrutable his ways . . . For from him and through him and to him are all things. To him be glory for ever.'[5]

4. Acts 10:34–35
5. Romans 11:33, 36

63. A Thousand Millions

Hebrews 12:1–2. *With all these witnesses to faith around us like a cloud, we must throw off every encumbrance, every sin to which we cling, and run with resolution the race for which we are entered, our eyes fixed on Jesus, on whom faith depends from start to finish.*

(N.E.B.)

O Christ, my Lord, you said that if you were lifted up on the cross you would draw all men unto you. You also said that as there could be no crop in nature without the death of the seed, so without your death there could be no harvest of souls. It did not take long, dear Lord, before the promise began to be fulfilled, for fifty days later three thousand souls came to believe in you, who in a few days would be journeying back to their own countries to report what had happened. Your love seen in the cross has warmed the hearts of people in every generation, and today there are a thousand million disciples. The former and the latter scriptures have been translated into over a thousand languages and your Church has been planted in every country.[1]

Your most loving disciple saw in vision what would happen, that the nations would come streaming into the city of God and saints from every race would be in the worshipping multitude around the throne of God, where you sit enthroned with him. The childlike and humble of heart, the loving of every race and religion will be there, numbered with the prophets and saints of every age. For as your most intimate disciple said, everyone who loves is born of God and knows God, though he may call the Father by a name unknown to us. Lord, I long that others may come to

1. John 12:24, 32

know you, to hear of your revelation of the heart of the Father and to find their own discoveries confirmed in you, and their deepest hopes fulfilled.[2]

Dear Lord, with nearly a third of the human race believing in you, your disciples ought to be more effective and the world ought to be a different place. If only we allowed our citizenship in your kingdom to inspire and influence our earthly citizenships, we should indeed be the salt of the earth, preserving, giving tone, sacrificing ourselves, permeating human society with grace. We should be fellow workers with you and the Father.[3]

If only we, your disciples, dear Lord, were more like you, if only people saw your grace operating in our lives, curbing our selfishness, making us more lovely, they would want to know the source of our changed lives.

Yet, Lord, I am comforted in the memory of the saints of every age, who with simple, childlike trust followed you, who wanted only to be and do and bear what your good loving will was for them, and to become like you, growing each day in holiness, love and maturity. Most of them were very much like us when they began, but kept their eyes on you and pressed on eagerly to the goal of perfection which you put before your disciples from the start, when you said that we must be perfect as our heavenly Father is perfect. I remember, too, dear Lord, your promise that when the disciple is fully taught he shall be like his master.[4]

There is also forgiveness, O Master, for failure, weakness, mistake, sin, and shortfall, which must go beyond the seventy times seven which you expected of Peter, redeeming the past, restoring the relationship with the Father and you, enabling us to go forward again with you.[5]

Beside all this, dear Lord, there is the assurance of your

2. Revelation 21:24–26; 1 John 4:7
3. Philippians 3:20; Matthew 5:13–14
4. Matthew 6:48; Luke 6:40
5. Matthew 18:22

grace, so often the prayer of Paul, something which he thought of as freely given by you, which can never be won in our own strength or deserved by our own achievement. Lord, I see that all we have to do is to open our inner being to your indwelling, allow your grace to direct and rule our hearts and keep us faithful to you. May the grace of you, our Lord Jesus Christ, be with us all, so that in the strength of what you have already done we may go forward to what you still want done for us and the whole world![6]

6. Romans 6:20; 1 Corinthians 16:32; Philippians 4:23; Philemon 25; Revelation 22:21

64. The Father's World

Romans 8:22. Up to the present, we know, the whole created universe groans in all its parts as if in the pangs of childbirth. (N.E.B.)

O Christ, my Lord, one of the earliest thinkers about the world believed that it was the Father's creation. He pictured it coming into existence in stages in six divine 'days', which perhaps were not our days of twenty-four hours. He was clear that the Father's original plan was good, and that everything that came from the creating energy of God was good, very good. The climax of creation was man, made in the Father's likeness and capable of communion with him. We see in you, dear Lord, man as the Father intended him to be.[1]

Even in those early days of religious consciousness it was clear that things had gone wrong. Man failed to live as the Father's child, seeing the Father's will as wise and good, needing to depend on the Father and not only on the activity of the mind. He needed the light that was in life itself, as well as his own knowledge, but tragically insisted on going his own way. Dear Lord, it is not difficult to see this in our hindsight of you when you lived our life in this gone-wrong world, in our relationship with you as the ever-living, ever-present one, and more sadly in our own heredity and waywardness.[2]

In the world in which we live today, there is much of beauty and wonder of which you were aware in Nazareth and Galilee. But there is also much cruelty in nature, though that seems to be instinctive and defensive whereas in man it

1. Genesis 1:31, 27
2. Genesis 3, 6:5; Romans 3:23

is deliberate and insatiably cruel. In natural phenomena too there are flaws like earthquakes, hurricanes, floods. Could it be, Lord, that the world is still unfinished, that creation is still going on? New galaxies, quasars, 'black holes' suggest that this may be so. Epidemics, congenital and at present incurable diseases, point in the same direction. In our age, dear Lord, men have such power in their own hands, to build or to destroy; it would seem that we need to become sub-creators with the Father and you.

In the gospel portraits we see you healing diseased and disabled bodies, deranged and imprisoned minds, divided and sick spirits – and everything we see you doing in time is what the Father is doing eternally. In John's vision of the things that shall be 'hereafter', he learns that 'God will wipe away every tear from their eyes'. He adds that as a result of God's presence with us, so evident in your earthly life, there shall be no more death, nor mourning, nor crying, nor any more pain. O dear Lord, the Father's Buddhist children will be thrilled in this, for the issue that moved the Buddha was the cause of suffering and the escape from it.[3]

So, dear Lord, the Father's world is still a world in travail, and its present sufferings are birthpangs, made more painful by delayed birth. You hinted this in your warnings about the inevitable fate of Jerusalem and the future of our race. Your servant Paul saw that the sufferings of his time were not to be compared with the glory and happiness that is the Father's will. But he saw, with you, the whole of creation groaning in travail together, waiting eagerly for the coming forward of the children of God to assist in its birth. Here and now, dear Lord, your disciples are to live in the values of the Kingdom, with love as our animating force and with the dedicated aim of helping you to build the Kingdom of the Father's love.[4]

In the confidence of this hope, would it be completely

3. Revelation 7:17, 21:4
4. Mark 13:8; John 1:4–5; Luke 21:34; Romans 8:22, 19

faithless to wonder if this new order will ever come in human history, that it will only come in the final consummation? You, Lord, taught us to pray that the Father's Kingdom should come on earth as it is in heaven. It could come, dear Lord, if the Father's name is honoured and his will done by men as by angels and saints in heaven. In the meantime we are to pray and work that it should. Your beloved disciple in his vision of what is going on in the spiritual realm saw that the kingdoms of this world are becoming the Kingdom of God and of you, his Christ.[5]

That it will come in some measure in this dimension of time and history, we most gladly hope and expect. More than that, we look forward to the great moment when creation will be completed, and you, dear Christ, will deliver the perfected Kingdom to the Father, when our perishable nature shall need no more change because it will have attained the imperishable, when death will be swallowed up in eternal life, and God will be all in all, everything to everyone.[6]

5. Matthew 6:9, 10; Revelation 12:10
6. 1 Corinthians 15:24, 53–54

65. Interpreting Each Present

John 16:12–13. *I still have many things to say to you but they would be too much for you now. But when the Spirit of truth comes he will lead you to the complete truth . . . and he will tell you of the things to come.* (J.B.)

O Christ, my Lord, you said that people were better at forecasting the weather than at interpreting the signs of the times and the significance of things that were happening. Your apostle Paul warned us that definite consequences follow our actions as naturally as reaping follows sowing. Help me, dear Master, to do good deeds now that will produce a harvest of goodness and blessing, and in the wisdom of your Spirit enable me to interpret the cause and meaning of events in the world.

O Christ, my Lord, I see how in every happening and new development you took the matter to the Father to discover its significance and the Father's will concerning it – in planning your ministry, in choosing your original disciples, in the impact of your power to heal, in people's desire to make you a nationalist leader, in the reference of John the Baptist's death, in the growing threat to yourself, in the painful moment of decision in Gethsemane, in the desolation of the cross.

Like the prophets before you, you saw the consequence of wrong decisions, actions and attitudes, the seeds of the present developing into a harvest for the future as when you wept over Jerusalem because its people did not see the day of opportunity and decision, a blindness that would inevitably lead to tragedy. And because you loved Jerusalem the pain was all the sharper. Yet like the prophets, dear Lord, you called for and hoped for a change of heart which would change the future and produce happiness and blessing.

O Christ of the Kingdom, let the Church be your prophet to the nations, warning people of dangers ahead, interpreting the consequences as well as deploring the immediate action. Let your priests be sensitive to the consequences in individual lives of wrong ways of living, as they exercise the care and cure of souls.

May we your followers today be conscious of the Father always at work to neutralize the evil, to strengthen the good, to redeem each situation and bring something good out of what seems to be pain and loss. May we your disciples so love the world that we will be ready to stand for the world, if necessary against the world, for the sake of the world. More even than that, may we be shown the positive saving activity of God's wise and loving will. Show us somehow, dear Lord, how to do the best possible deeds in even the worst of times.

And, dear Master, don't let us be blind to the amount of goodness in the world, in thoughtful courageous leaders and in the basic goodness of many ordinary people. Let us see that those who work for good must be as disciplined, as shrewd and committed as those who work for worldly things.

Lord, I am slowly learning from you that goodness is the basic, the original and eternal, and that evil is the negative, the intruding and the impermanent. Strengthen this conviction, O Master, and keep me in touch with the source of all truth, goodness and love, that I may work with you and the Father, and have your compassion in the sight of all that is contrary, misguided, negative and destructive.

Matthew 16:2–3; Galatians 6:7–10; John 12:24, 16:13

PART X

Disciple's Devotion

66. Transfigured With You

2 Corinthians 3:18. *We, with our unveiled faces reflecting like mirrors the brightness of the Lord, all grow brighter and brighter as we are turned into the image that we reflect.* (J.B.)

Lord, it was while you were praying that your three watching disciples saw the glory shine through, your face bright with joy and an aura of light clothing your body. In their hearts rose the conviction that you were God's beloved Son and that the secret of life was to listen to you and obey you.

It was as if you were conferring with unseen companions. Afterwards you must have told them that this was indeed so, that the two figures were Moses and Elijah and that the subject was the crisis ahead.

Moses had brought Israel to God in covenant on Mount Sinai. Elijah had kept them faithful in the struggle against false gods and mistaken faith on Mount Carmel. Were you comforted in the assurance that they were living still, and concerned in your mission? Did you feel assured that you too would not be destroyed by death, that your God and their God, your Father and their Father was the God of the living? Did you once again accept the probable cross, the way of sacrifice, as you did in the forty days down by the Jordan?

O my Lord, let me see the glory, let me hear the voice from the overshadowing cloud that veiled the Vision.

Lord, you want us to be transfigured, as Moses was when he came down from Sinai after his forty days, like you, with God. The waiting people saw the brightness in his face, something of the reflection and serenity of the Father. Help me through our experience of that glory to be changed into the divine likeness from one degree of glory to another.

Dear Lord, it may not be spiritually safe for us to know this, but perhaps others may perceive that we have been with you and the Father.

Let me be assured, dear Master, from my experience of your moment of transfiguration, and be strengthened to be and do and bear all that is the Father's will for me, and finally come to the heavenly Zion, the city of the living God, to the innumerable company of angels, to the spirits of just men made perfect, to the judge who is God of all, and to you, the mediator and go-between, who came from the heart of the Father to take us there with you for ever.

Mark 9:2–8; Luke 9:28–36; Matthew 17:1–8; Mark 12:26–27; Exodus 34:29–32; 2 Corinthians 3:18; Hebrews 13:22–24

67. Always a Learner

Psalm 119:103. *How sweet are thy words to my taste, sweeter than honey to my mouth!* (R.S.V.)

O Christ, my Lord, as years go by I learn that I am always only a disciple, a learner in your school of holiness and love, never ceasing to learn something new from you about the Father whom you have taught me to love, something new about the meaning and goal of life, with new experiences of your grace, the inner eye being enlightened to see you constantly at the Father's work within myself and in the new dimension in which you call me to live and love.

You teach me that you are perceived and understood not so much by the effects of the mind but by love, which engenders a deep simple relationship. When you examine me with penitent Peter – 'Do you really love me?' – my heart replies with him, 'Lord, you know that I love you, help me to love you more and more, until I love you with the whole of my being.' 'Abide in me and let me abide in you,' you urge and plead, and there are times when we are merged and united, and I learn that I can do nothing apart from you, but that with you nothing is impossible. Everything of spiritual value is begun, continued and ended in you, dear Master.[1]

You teach me that I must put you first and above everyone and everything else, far above family even, and I find that when I do this I love them more than before, more deeply, imaginatively and creatively, wanting your good, loving and wise will for them, discovering that you love them more even than I do, and that you desire their true

1. John 15:4; Philippians 4:13

happiness more than I do.[2]

It is not easy, dear Lord, to discover your will, always identical with the Father's will. You simplify matters for me when you say that if I would be your disciple, all I have to do is to follow you.

You are the Way, expressed in personal terms rather than in a set of rigid rules. With that understanding, I begin to see that with your loving heart there are many ways of doing your will in actual situations, more than just one thing to say when words are needed. I am learning slowly, dear Lord, that it is as I grow more like you that what I am is the answer, and that I begin to forget even that. Perhaps that is what you meant when you said that the disciple must deny himself. And you added that he must take up his cross and follow you, repudiating self-will and subtle self-interest, even the satisfaction of being pleased with himself and satisfied with his progress in discipleship. Lord, you do search out the hidden corners of the heart. Once the disciple hears you knocking at the door of the heart and lets you enter, he had better be aware of what he is in for. You will want to look into every room of the house of the soul, including the attic where we keep all our rubbish and the cellar where we bury the shameful things.[3]

You assure me that you are with your disciples always; there is no place where I may go, no circumstances in which I may find myself, no happenings which may come upon me, when you are not present, in spite of my falterings of faith and periods of darkness. Help me to know, dear Lord, from your own hours of darkness, that faith is most faith when it is being tempested, travailed, tempted. Let me remember your promise that I shall not be overcome, that in all things I can be more than victorious in and through you, and that nothing can separate me from the Father's love. Help me to have this faith, not for myself alone, but

2. Luke 14:26
3. Luke 14:27; Revelation 3:20

for those whom I love, and for every other child of the Father.[4]

You teach me further, Lord, that my love, like yours, must extend to everyone, there must be no limit. My neighbour whom the Father commands me to love as myself, is everyone, because all are his children, equally and eternally dear, without barriers of race or culture or education or wealth or poverty. I must be open and welcoming to everyone, as you were and are. You tell me, Master, that I must love even my enemies or those I think to be so. You tell me that I don't have to respond to people as they act to me; I mustn't be conditioned by how they behave to me, but be free to love. Keep on teaching me this lesson, dear Lord, convince me that where there is no love, I must pour love in, so that I and others may draw love out.[5]

Dear Master, you can see that I shall always be a disciple and never be able to do without you. Let my desire never rise above this or fall below it.

4. Romans 8:37–39
5. Matthew 5:43–48

68. Trembling Disciple

John 14:1. *Set your troubled hearts at rest. Trust in God always; trust also in me.* (N.E.B.)

O Christ, my Lord, I am grateful that your first disciples needed assurance and encouragement, for I too am often afraid of your demands and of my own inadequacy, and of the criticisms of others. Like Peter in the stormy sea, I look at the waves and my faith fails, instead of keeping my eye on your coming towards me in the storm. I fear that at the end you may reproach me: 'O man of little faith, why did you doubt?'

In the thought of your holiness and love I cry out with Peter, 'Depart from me, for I am a sinful man, O Lord,' though like him I would be heartbroken if you took me at my word.

You hold before me the perfection of the Father as my goal, and I know how far short I fall of that eternal standard.

Sometimes I see you striding ahead of me into encounter with opposition and trouble, and I tremble for my own courage and your expectation. Let me never fear, dear Lord, as long as I occasionally glimpse you ahead.

Dear Master, when I think of some of your martyrs today and of fellow men suffering for truth and integrity, and see the inhuman cruelty inflicted upon them, I shudder at my own fear of pain and tremble for my faithfulness. Open my eyes, dear Lord, as you did with your very first martyr, Stephen, to see you standing in the Father's presence to strengthen every witness for truth.

Master, I am rather like the one-talent man in your parable, afraid to lose it and afraid to use it. When I think of the divine judgement on my life, I tremble, but you assure me that the Father sent you to save and not to condemn. And if you are the judge, I know that there will be understanding and mercy, and that you will plead excuse for me.

Lord, like your two ambitious disciples I am eager for honour, recognition from the world and approval from you. You whisper to me, 'Can you drink the cup involved in each ambition and vocation?' Lord, it is easy to answer with them, 'I can,' when the heart is warm with devotions. Help me, dear Lord, to see clearly the cost of being your disciple and not to grudge it. If you put a cup to my lips help me to take it, trustingly, knowing that you will also give the strength to drink it and find it a cup of salvation and blessing.

Lord, I remember the dismay of those first disciples when you warned them that one of them was not heart-whole in his loyalty, and their troubled question, 'Lord, is it I?' I do not want to betray you, dear Lord, either willingly or unknowingly. Help me to ask their question in sincerity and truth, and then assure me that my troubled asking is a sign that I want to be heart-whole as your disciple, and that your grace is sufficient for every test.

I tremble at the inevitable thought of death, help me to find you in death also, and to be reborn into the spiritual and the eternal, the sphere of more life and love.

Lord, I am a trembling disciple, but I want to be your disciple. Let my repeated prayer be that of an earlier believer: 'Though I am sometimes afraid, yet put I my trust in thee!'

Mark 10:32–34; Matthew 14:28–31; Luke 5:8; John 7:16–17; Mark 10:35–45; Matthew 26:20–25; Psalm 56:3

69. Never Enough

Philippians 3:12. *Not that I have become perfect yet: I have not yet won, but I am still running, trying to capture the prize for which Christ Jesus captured me.*
(J.B.)

O Christ, my Lord, you tell your disciples that we must be perfect as our heavenly Father is, an almost impossible task, certainly in our own strength, and difficult even with your grace – not that your grace is insufficient, but that our response is so weak. Even then, dear Lord, you tell us that in your grace we are more than conquerors and that when we are at our weakest it gets its greatest opportunity.

You endorse the greatest commandment of the divine Law, that we should love God with all our being, with all our mind, throughout our life and with all our will. Dear Lord, you know how far short we fall of this perfection.

You tell us that it is not enough to love our neighbour as ourself but as you love us. Only so, you say, can we be your disciples.

In your Sermon on the Mount, the fulfilled Law of the Kingdom, the new Law in the heart, you set before your disciples the ideal. Lord, we need constant help and frequent forgiveness as we try to live in this spirit. You tell us that when the law of men demands a legal mile of service, we must be ready to go a second mile of willing and free citizenship.

You are brutally frank with would-be disciples and insist that there can be no reservations. Dear Lord, if I ask, 'What do I still lack?' I know that you will put your finger on the very thing I want to keep, but I know too that you will look on me with eyes of love, as you did with the eager young man who first asked that rash question.

Lord, help me to be like your apostle Paul and never to think that I am nearing perfection, but to press on towards the upward call which our Father has made known to me through you, straining with all my strength towards the goal. Lord, I am like your earlier disciple Peter, and think that I have done extremely well if I forgive others seven times their real or supposed injustices to me, and you tell me that seventy times seven is not enough.

O Master, I pray with one of your recent disciples:

Dear Lord, let me never think that I have knowledge enough to need no teaching, wisdom enough to need no correction, talents enough to need no grace, goodness enough to need no progress, humility enough to need no penitence, strength enough without your Spirit.

O dear Lord, let me never become self-satisfied, never let me go, never despair of me, never abandon me, but continue your goading, sanctifying, life-giving, love-fulfilling work until I come closer to your hopes and will for me, until I begin to share your mind and love with something of your love, now in this life and beyond in your eternity.

Matthew 6:48; Luke 9:57–62; 2 Corinthians 3:4–6, 12:7–9; Philippians 3:12–16; Matthew 18:21–22; Hebrews 12:1–2; Eric Milner-White

70. Disciple's Litany

1.

Jesus meek and humble of heart:
   Hear me.
From the love of being esteemed:
   Deliver me, Jesus.
From the desire of being loved:
From the desire of being sought after:
From the desire of being honoured:
From the desire of being praised:
From the desire of being preferred to others:
From the desire of being consulted:
From the desire of being approved:
From the desire of being valued:
   Deliver me, Jesus.

2.

From the fear of being humbled:
   Deliver me, Jesus.
From the fear of being despised:
From the fear of suffering rebuffs:
From the fear of being misunderstood:
From the fear of being forgotten:
From the fear of being ridiculed:
From the fear of being injured:
From the fear of being suspected:
   Deliver me, Jesus.

3.

From the paralysis of unforgiven guilt:
  Liberate me, dear Lord.
From inner division and divided loyalty:
From a fear of responsibility:
From a hidden sense of inferiority:
From a fear of failure:
From a pride that refuses grace:
From every root of bitterness:
From every centre but the Father:
  Liberate me, dear Lord.

4.

That others may be more loved than I:
  Jesus, grant me the grace to wish.
That others may increase in this world's esteem
  And I diminish:
That others may be employed
  And I set aside:
That others may be preferred
  Before me in everything:
That others may be more holy than I:
That I may be as holy as thou wouldst have me be:
  Jesus, grant me the grace to wish.

5.

For the joy of knowing the Father and you:
  Train me, dear Master.
For growth towards your fullness:
For freedom to love others:
For the Father's wise and loving will:

For serenity in all that happens:
For faithfulness in your Church:
For helping to build the Father's world:
For eternal blessedness:
  Train me, dear Master.

(Parts 1, 2 and 4 are taken from Archbishop Goodier's, *The Life That Is Light*, Burns and Oates Ltd)

PART XI

A Writer's Prayer

A Writer's Prayer

For every sentence, clause and word,
That's not inlaid with thee, my Lord,
Forgive me, God, and blot each line
Out of my book, that is not thine.
But if, 'mongst all, thou find'st here one
Worthy thy benediction;
That one of all the rest shall be
The glory of my work, and me.

Robert Herrick, 1591–1674